Allegedly

The Hugh Brown Chainsaw Collection

Allegedly

The Hugh Brown Chainsaw Collection

Grand Central Press

ALLEGEDLY...

Some information you should know about Hugh Brown and this exhibition.

I have heard a number of rumors about this exhibition *Allegedly: The Hugh Brown Chainsaw Collection.* I have heard that Brown discovered a little known anomaly: dozens of celebrated artists throughout the twentieth century have, for some inexplicable reason, created artworks that include images of or make reference to chainsaws. Upon this discovery, Brown began buying all such images he could find to put together the collection on view here. This scenario is the least plausible of any explanation I have heard.

Another explanation is that upon learning about Brown's penchant for contemporary art and chainsaws, several unscrupulous art dealers plotted to defraud him. These dealers hired expert forgers to meticulously produce "chainsaw" artworks by famous artists. While I find this explanation more likely than the former, I find another explanation that is even more likely:

Hugh Brown created this hoax!

After meeting Brown and speaking to him on several occasions, I would not be surprised to learn that any of the above explanations are true. However, for a number of reasons, I believe Brown is responsible for this deception.

Brown has the experience and background to accurately fabricate work by other artists. He was an award-winning Creative Director at Rhino Records from 1997 to 2008–he won three Grammys® and a host of other awards. He was well known for his inventive sculptural CD-compilation box sets.

But why would Brown go to such trouble? Appropriation has always been a part of the art world. As Picasso put it, "great artists steal" (the implication being that lesser artists only borrow). Duchamp drew a mustache on a reproduction of the Mona Lisa. Shortly after the beginning of pop art, a blatant phenomenon of wholesale replication of art emerged in the 60s and pretty much peaked in the late 70s and early 80s. But these artists were ripping off other artists to make high-minded statements about perception and commodification of art. None of these artists included chainsaws in their art; they would have found this gratuitous at best. I don't think Brown's motives here are that lofty.

Brown strikes me more as someone who's trying to throw a monkey wrench—I guess that should be chainsaw—into the whole art world star system. I don't think this is malicious. I believe Brown genuinely likes the artists who are, one way or another, exploited in this show. He also likes chainsaws.

In any event, in this exhibition we get to see passionately constructed artworks that if not created by famous artists look so much like their art that it begs the question: What's the difference? And we have to wonder: What's with the chainsaws?

MIKE McGEE
Gallery Director, Cal State Fullerton

A SMALL SAMPLING OF OTHER ITEMS FROM THE COLLECTION

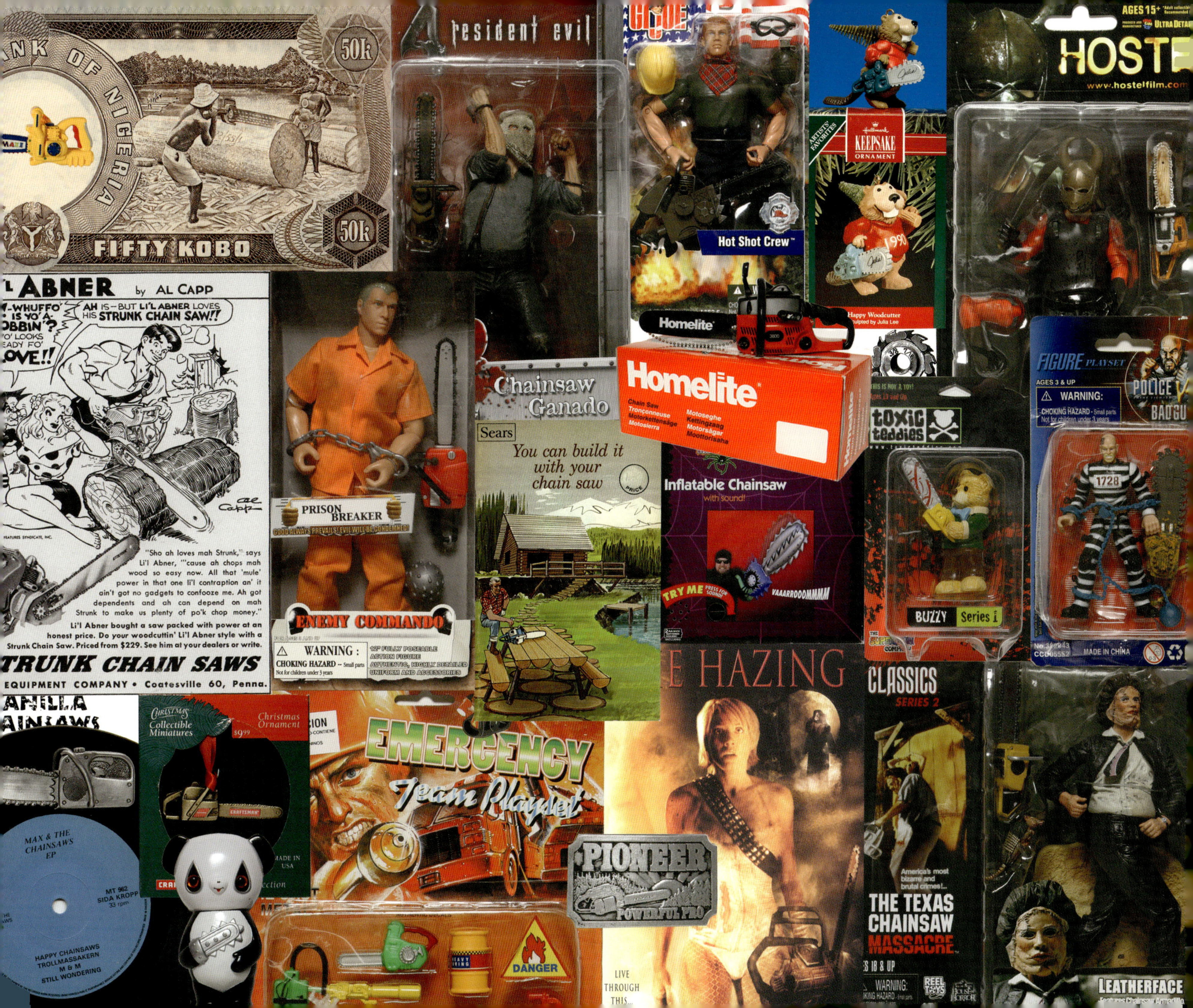

FIFTY KOBO
50k
resident evil
Hot Shot Crew™
KEEPSAKE ORNAMENT
Happy Woodcutter
HOSTEL
www.hostelfilm.com
ABNER by AL CAPP
AH IS—BUT LI'L ABNER LOVES HIS STRUNK CHAIN SAW!!
"Sho ah loves mah Strunk," says Li'l Abner, "'cause ah chops mah wood so easy now. All that 'mule' power in that one li'l contraption an' it ain't got no gadgets to confooze me. Ah got dependents and ah can depend on mah Strunk to make us plenty of po'k chop money."
Li'l Abner bought a saw packed with power at an honest price. Do your woodcuttin' Li'l Abner style with a Strunk Chain Saw. Priced from $229. See him at your dealers or write.
TRUNK CHAIN SAWS
EQUIPMENT COMPANY • Coatesville 60, Penna.
PRISON BREAKER
ENEMY COMMANDO
WARNING:
CHOKING HAZARD
Chainsaw Ganado
Sears
You can build it with your chain saw
Homelite
Inflatable Chainsaw
with sound!
TRY ME
VAAARROOOMMMM
toxic teddies
BUZZY Series 1
FIGURE PLAYSET
POLICE
WARNING:
1728
MADE IN CHINA
E HAZING
CLASSICS
SERIES 2
THE TEXAS CHAINSAW MASSACRE
LEATHERFACE
Christmas Ornament
Collectible Miniatures
MAX & THE CHAINSAWS EP
HAPPY CHAINSAWS
TROLLMASSAKERN
STILL WONDERING
EMERGENCY
Team Playset
PIONEER
DANGER
LIVE THROUGH THIS

ACTUALLY...

Some information you should know about Hugh Brown and this exhibition.

I know what you're going to say when you see Hugh Brown's mixed-media series *Allegedly.* You're going to say "this is art about chainsaws." But you'll be wrong. This is not art about chainsaws; this is art about obsession. A brief recap of Brown's life and work make it clear that he's been an obsessive—a very hip obsessive—since he was a child, and that, of course, he wound up making a complicated body of work about chainsaws. What else would he do?

Brown was born in Saginaw, Michigan, in 1954, and moved to the Chicago suburbs at the age of seven. His earliest art memories include hours spent at his grandparents' house, when he was around eight years old, poring over books of cartoons from the New Yorker. He was particularly fond of Peter Arno and Charles Addams, and Brown cites Addams as his first favorite artist. That's pretty sophisticated for an eight-year-old.

Brown had the advantage of growing up in one of America's great art cities, and his official art education commenced soon thereafter. "When I was around thirteen I remember going to the Art Institute of Chicago and being knocked out by an alcove filled with giant paintings by Ivan Albright. Albright made the paintings of the deteriorating man for the film *The Picture of Dorian Gray*, and there's amazing detail in his work. I remember the painted spider webs, and the lace in a few of the pieces—really beautiful and mysterious," Brown recalls of Albright's magnificently creepy work.

As a high school student Brown began collecting records obsessively. He also became a regular fixture on the local music scene, and began buying art. Psychedelic and Op art, works by Peter Max, propaganda posters from World War II—he compiled quite a kooky hodge-podge of stuff. After graduating from high school, his collecting moved up a notch, and he started buying lithographs, screen prints, and photography. Brown was deeply involved with popular culture by the time he began classes at UC Berkeley, but he hadn't yet figured out what his place in it would be.

While pursuing degrees in psychology and criminology, Brown spent his leisure time photographing the concerts he was constantly attending; he didn't know it at the time, but this was the beginning of the path that would allow him to flourish as an artist. Brown spent the mid 70s in England, studying psychology and international law at the University of Sussex, and while he was there the first rumblings of punk rock began to be heard. During his time in England he acquired darkroom and silk-screening skills, and began making T-shirts printed with his photographs for his friends; by the time he returned to Berkeley he'd become extremely proficient in the darkroom.

This brings us to 1976 and punk rock, which is when Brown really found his métier; punk was perfectly tailored to Brown's aesthetic, which had always leaned toward the subversive and cheeky. For evidence of that, look no further than his business card.

"In Berkeley I used to hang out at a record store called Rather Ripped, and I saw Patti Smith perform there in the mid 70s," Brown remembers. "I became friends with Patti's manager, Jane Friedman, and took lots of photographs of Patti, many of which I made into T-shirts. Whenever a New York band came to San

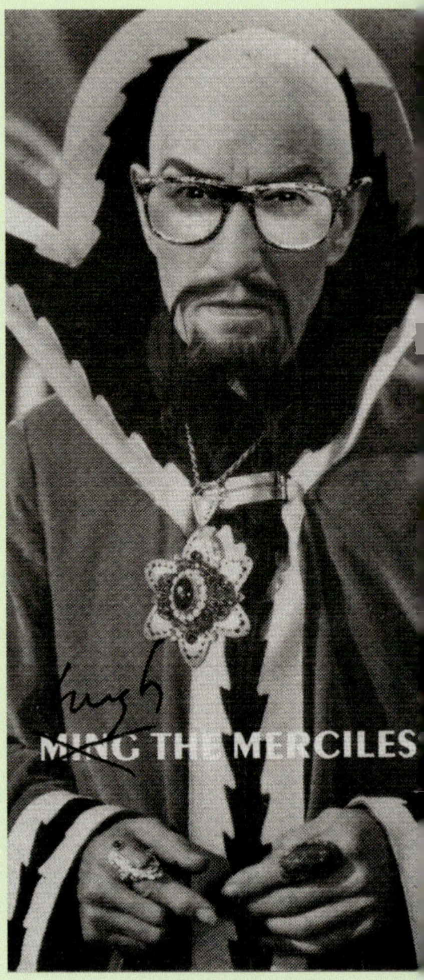

Francisco, Jane would arrange for me to meet them, and I made T-shirts using my photographs of loads of musicians. Around that time people started asking me to do record covers, too. My first big cover came about when Sandy Pearlman was in San Francisco producing the second Clash album, *Give Em Enough Rope,* and he invited me to the studio to photograph the band. At the time, I had an exhibition up at this place called Postcard Palace, and the show featured pieces incorporating altered Chinese propaganda imagery. One of the pieces included a postcard of a dead cowboy with a vulture on his back titled *End of the Road… for the Cowboy Imperialist,* and when Mick and Joe came to the show and saw it they decided to use the image for their album cover."

Brown went on to build a reputation as one of the most innovative graphic designers in the world of alternative music. As creative director of I.R.S. Records, from 1989 through 1995, and Rhino Records, from 1996 through 2007, Brown was responsible for some of the most memorable imagery to come out of the music business prior to its recent implosion. If you're even remotely cool, you'll find his name if you look through your CD collection.

Did I mention that Brown is one of the busiest multitaskers you're likely to encounter? He always has several projects going, in various stages of development, and chainsaws have been on his mind for quite a while. "I began collecting chainsaw related stuff in the early 80s," he recalls. "Then, one Saturday in 1986, I acquired three different chainsaw items in one day: I got a trucker hat with a saw, an earring, and a comic book cover. The next day I opened

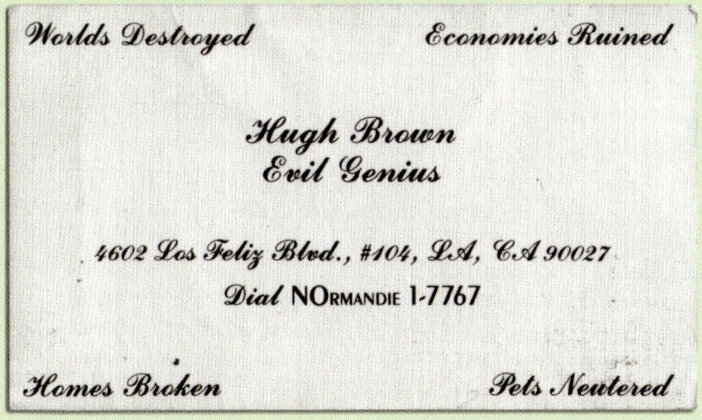

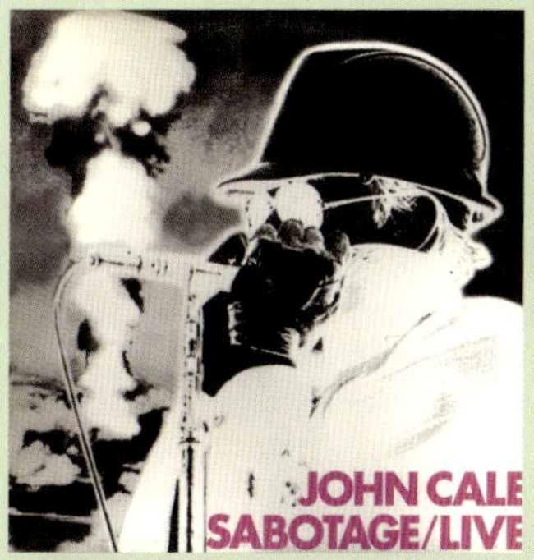

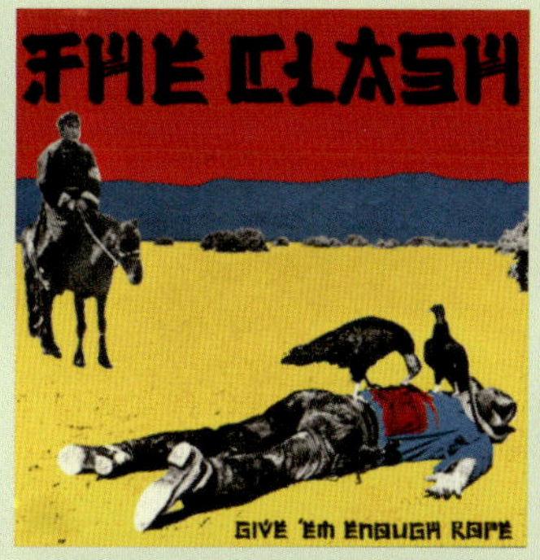

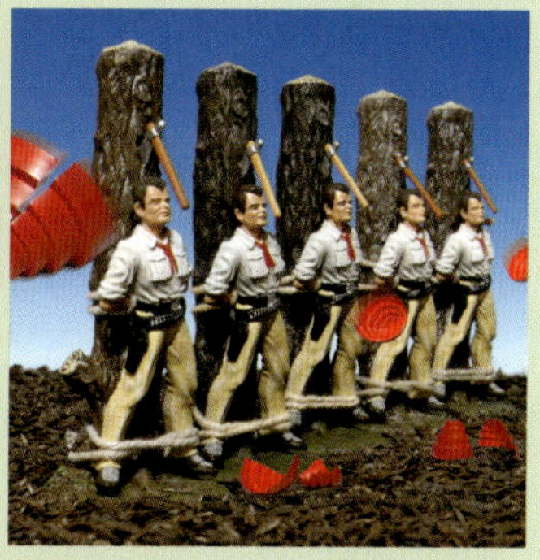

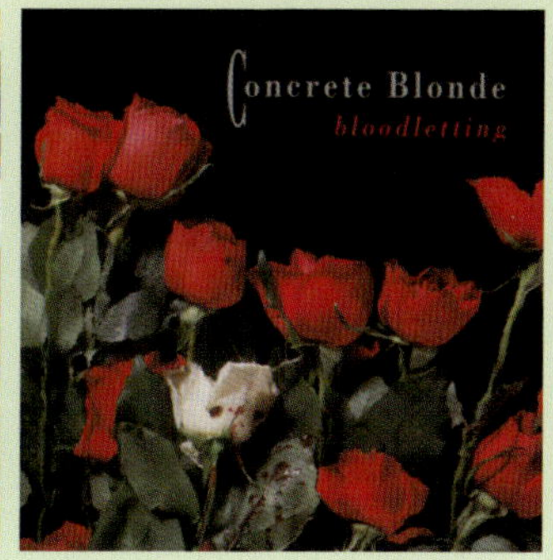

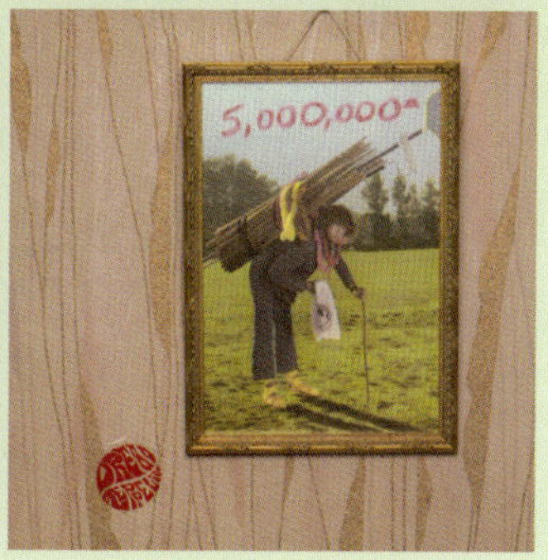

the Sunday paper and out fell the Sears' lawn and garden section with an ad for chainsaws on the cover. I took that as a sign from God, and thus began the coffee table book, *Saw: The Chainsaw in Popular Culture.*"

At that point Brown produced his first piece—a delicate wire sculpture executed in the manner of Alexander Calder—but he then got sidetracked. This can happen with Brown, and his chainsaw project took a twenty-year time out. During the 90s he produced a few more homages/forgeries, (the viewer can decide for him or herself which is the appropriate word), but it wasn't until 2007 that he was again seized with chainsaw fever; once it struck he produced forty more pieces in just eighteen months.

Chainsaws are as low culture as it gets, but the way Brown uses them is very stealthy and inside; you need to know a lot about art, and specific artists, to grasp precisely how he's riffing on them. His work is not simple. Moreover, it's extremely labor intensive. With a few exceptions, these images were not constructed in the computer: Brown actually made all these art works—and this is where the obsessive part kicks in. He made every effort for his pieces to have as much fidelity to the original as possible, and the research he did for this series is an artwork unto itself. What kind of fur did Meret Oppenheim use on her famous Surrealist teacup? (Chinese Antelope). What brand of gouache did Matisse use for his Jazz series (Linel). Brown knows the answers to these esoteric questions, and he knows lots of other things, too.

He made it his business to know that the dye transfer process Harold Edgerton used in his photographs is long gone, as are the ingredients for the Carbro printing process central to work by Paul Outerbridge. Brown was unable to produce authentic Yves Klein Blue, because the original ingredients are highly toxic and banned, nor could he find a facility capable of producing a nine-foot silkscreen for his Barbara Kruger piece. The computer did come in handy for a few works: his John Baldessari was created entirely in the computer, and his Berenice Abbott *Spinning Chainsaw* was pieced together in Photoshop as well. This isn't to suggest that Brown looks for shortcuts. Are you kidding? He prefers doing things the hard way. To make his Bruce Nauman neon he tracked down and used the same fabricator Bruce used. He didn't even attempt his Jackson Pollock until he'd spent hours studying and practicing Pollock's wrist movements as captured in the famous footage by Hans Namuth.

This diligent research is one of the most beautiful parts of Brown's work. He respects art enough to gather every last shred of information about it, but he never loses sight of the fact that the fundamental function of art is pleasure. Brown has fun with the art he loves; he interacts with it, dismantles then reassembles it, and he allows us to listen in on the conversation. It's a pretty funny conversation, too, but if you listen hard enough you'll also detect a touch of devotion.

KRISTINE McKENNA
Los Angeles-based writer and curator, July 2009

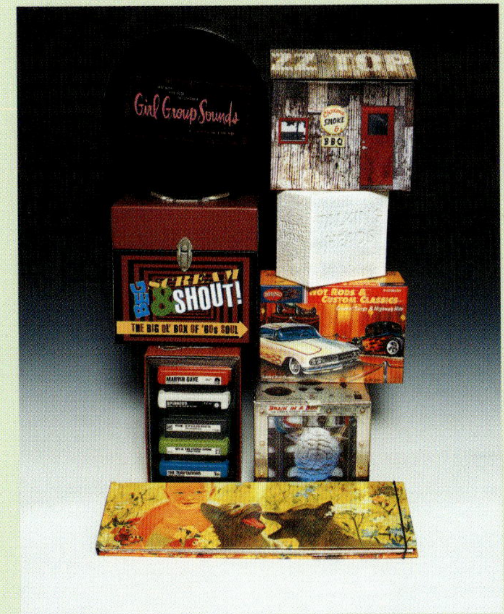

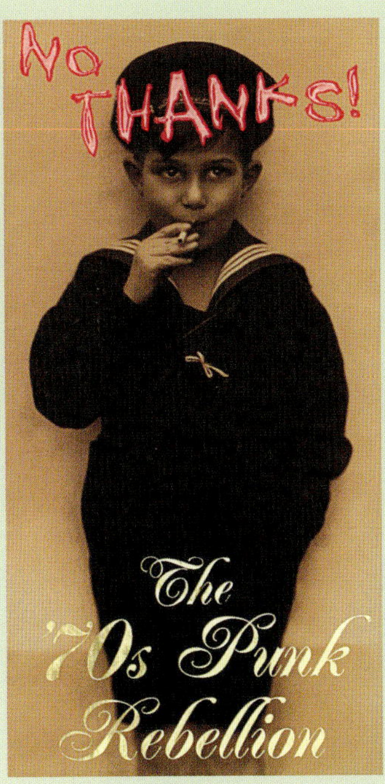

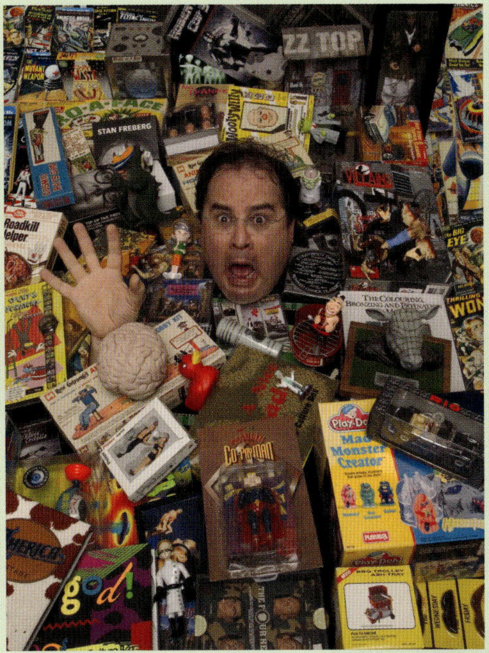

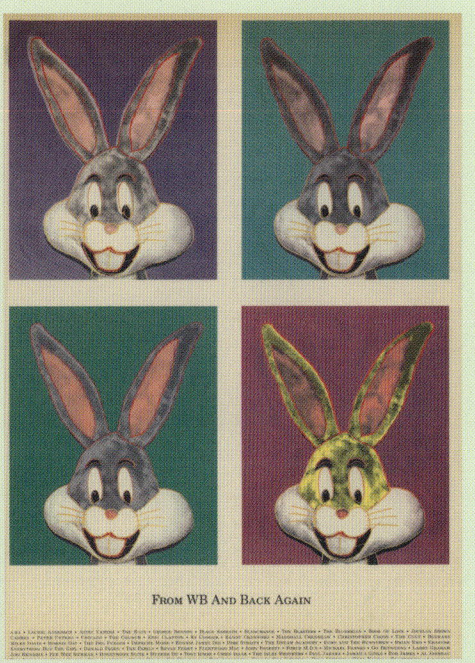

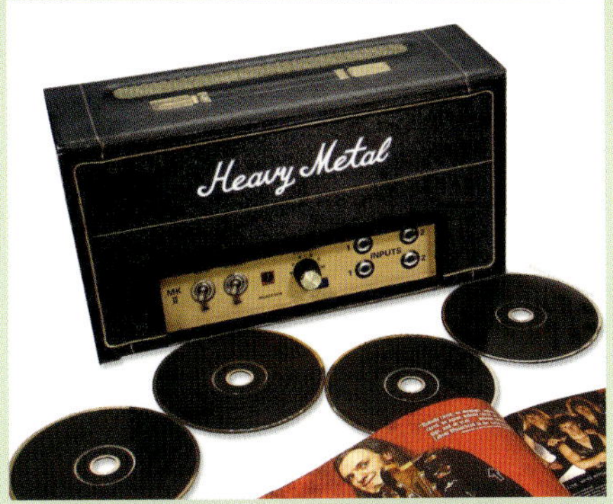

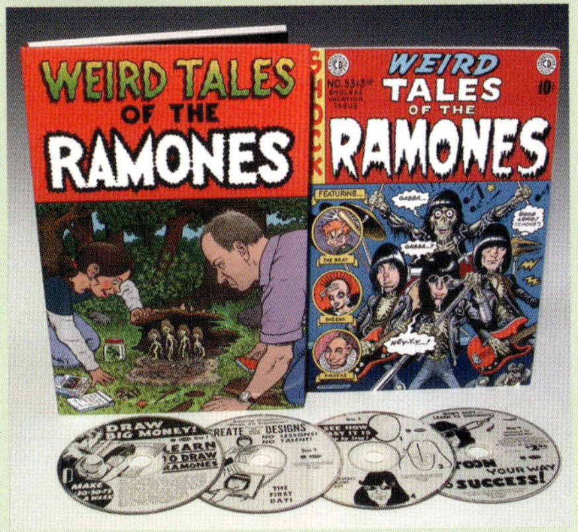

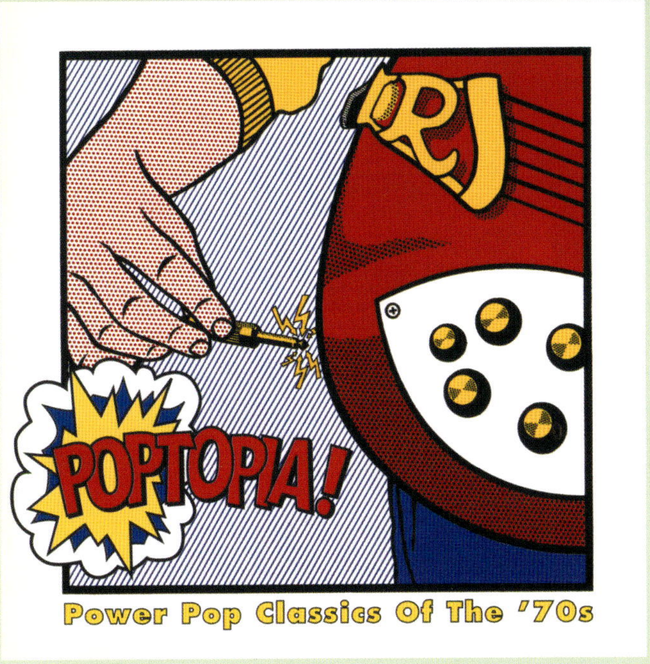

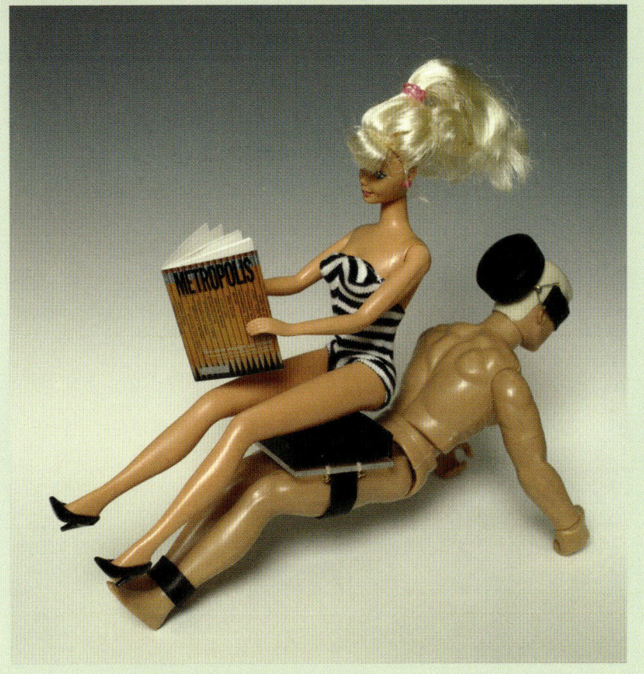

Clockwise from bottom left. Various Rhino box sets — self-portrait — Warner ad for Warhol's ***Interview***

The Joe Chair, finalist in Metropolis'/Vitra's ***Design the Perfect Chair for Barbie*** competition (with John Heiden) — ***Poptopia***

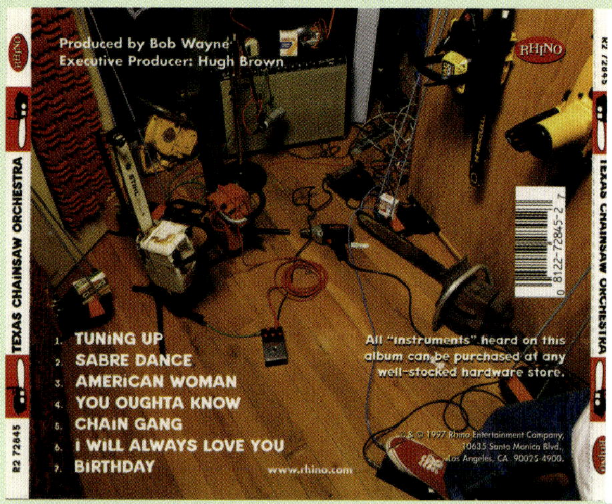

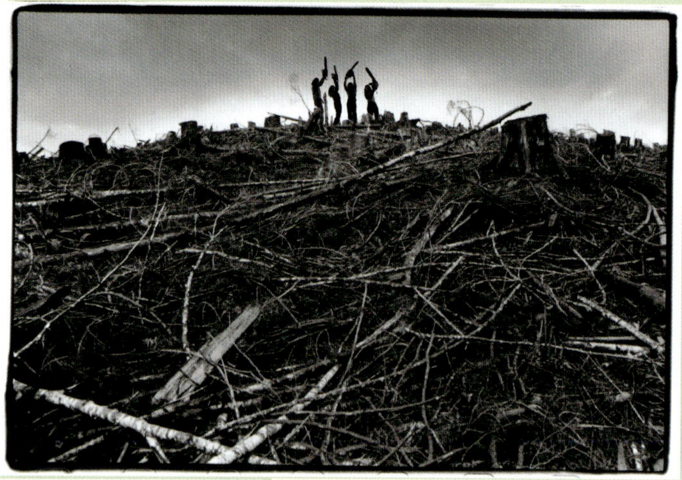

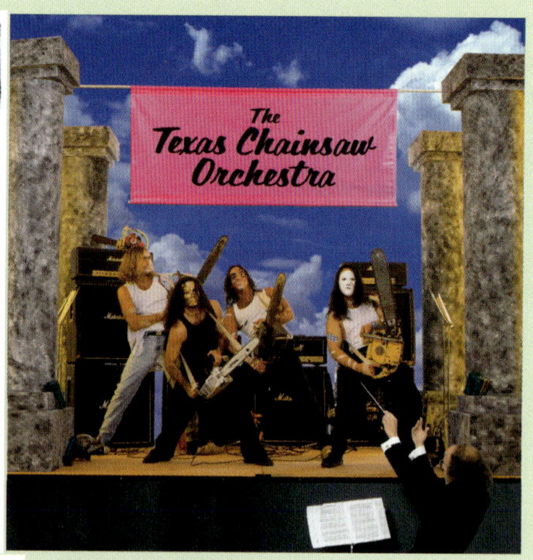

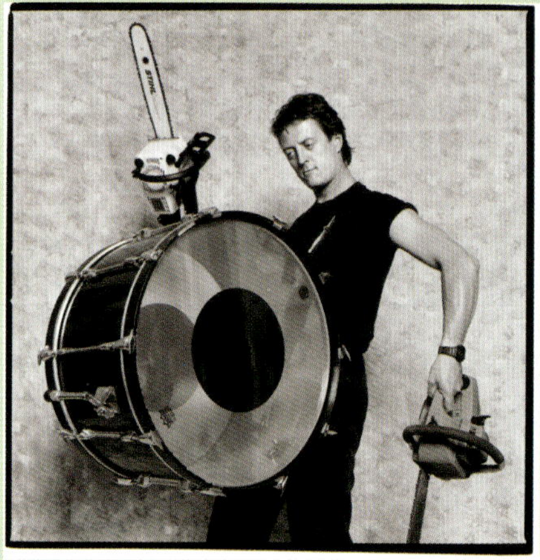

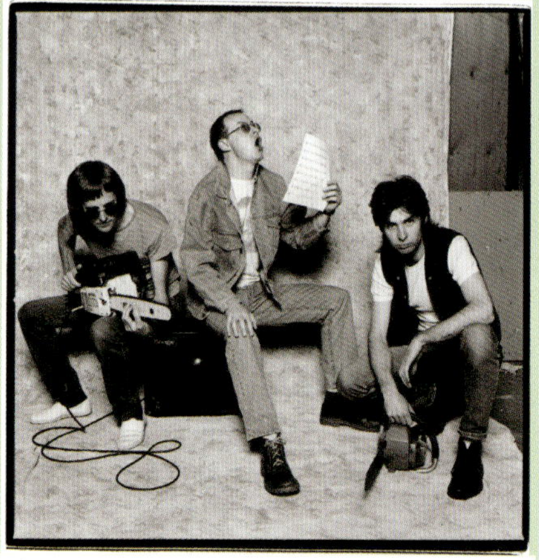

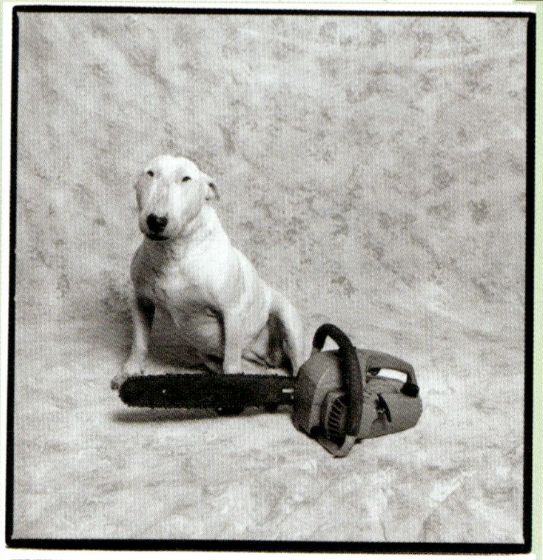

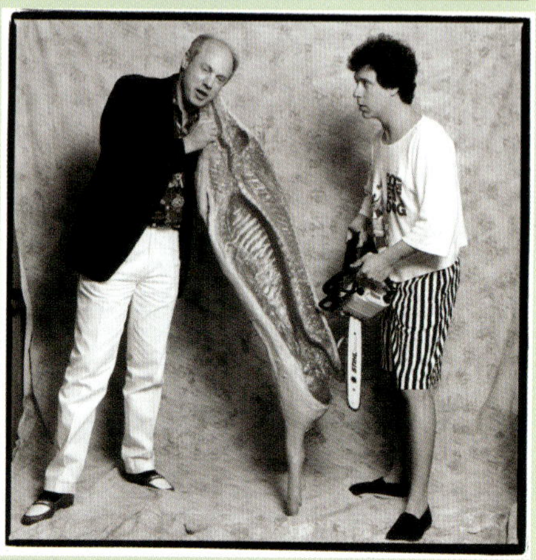

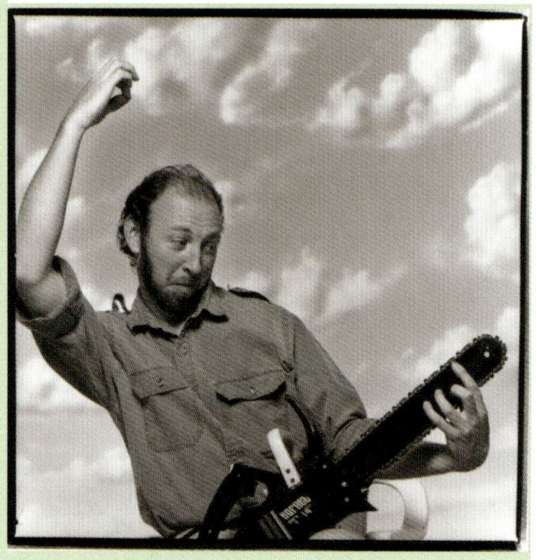

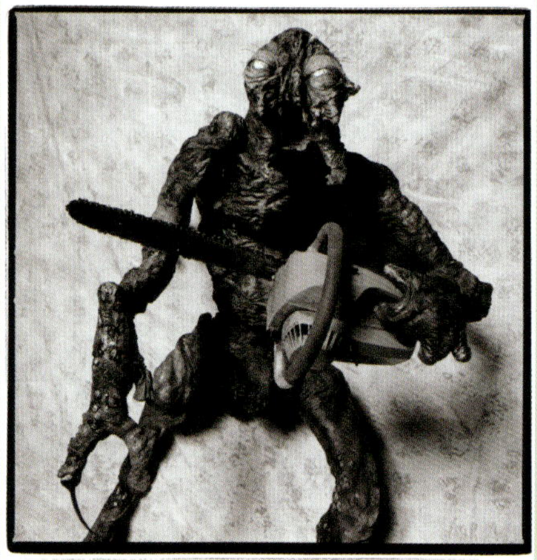

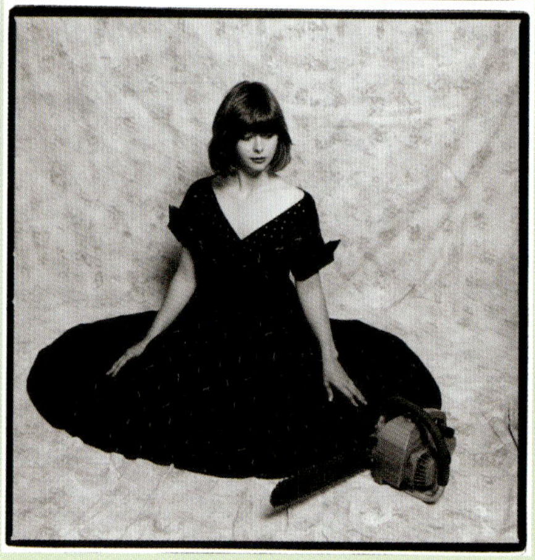

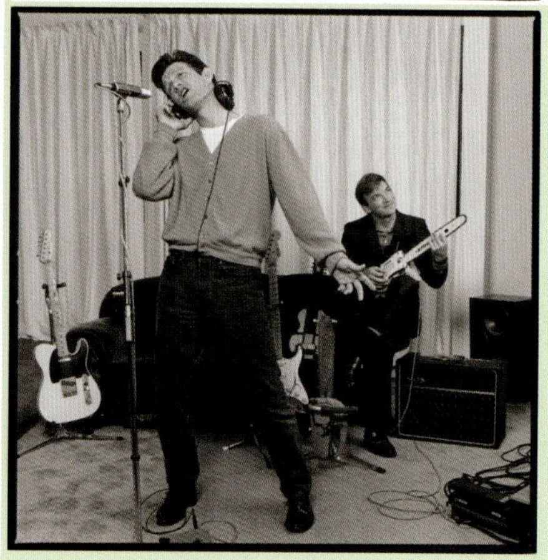

Top. Texas Chainsaw Orchestra CD. — *Middle.* Prairie Prince, XTC, Ray Charles, The Durocs, (Ron Nagel/Scott Mathews). — *Bottom.* Richard Thompson, The Fly, Jenni Muldaur, Chris Issac & Jimmy Wilsey

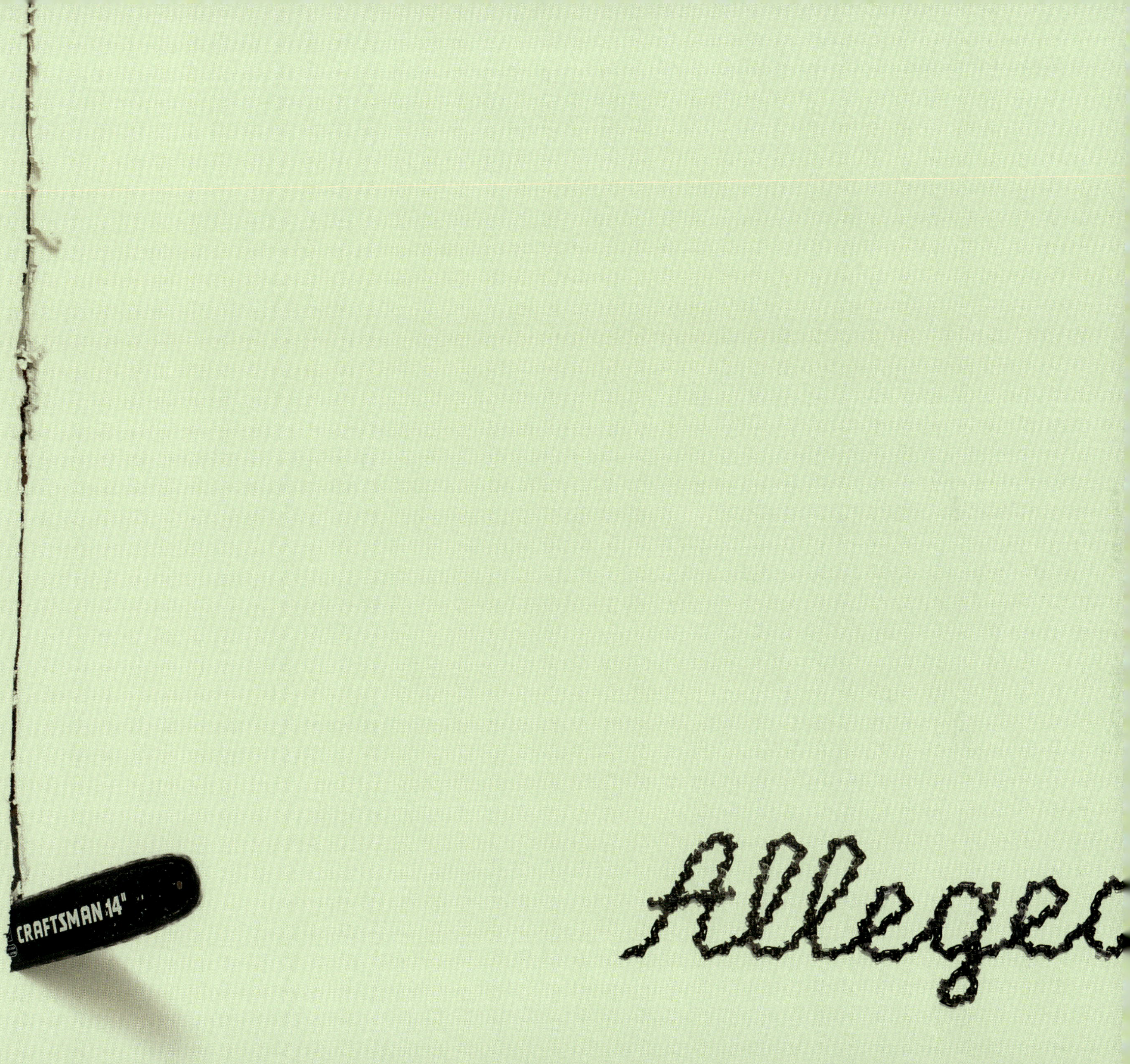
CRAFTSMAN 14"
Allege

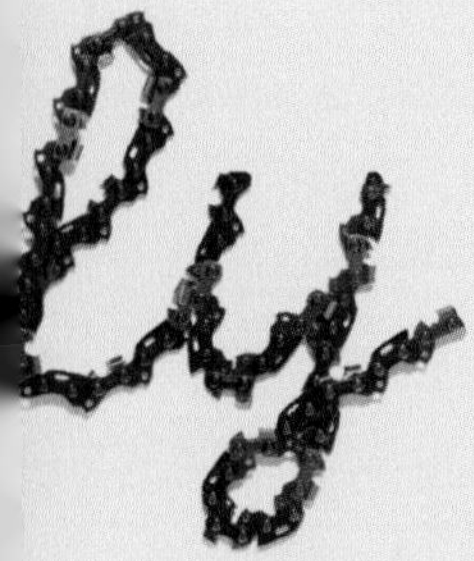

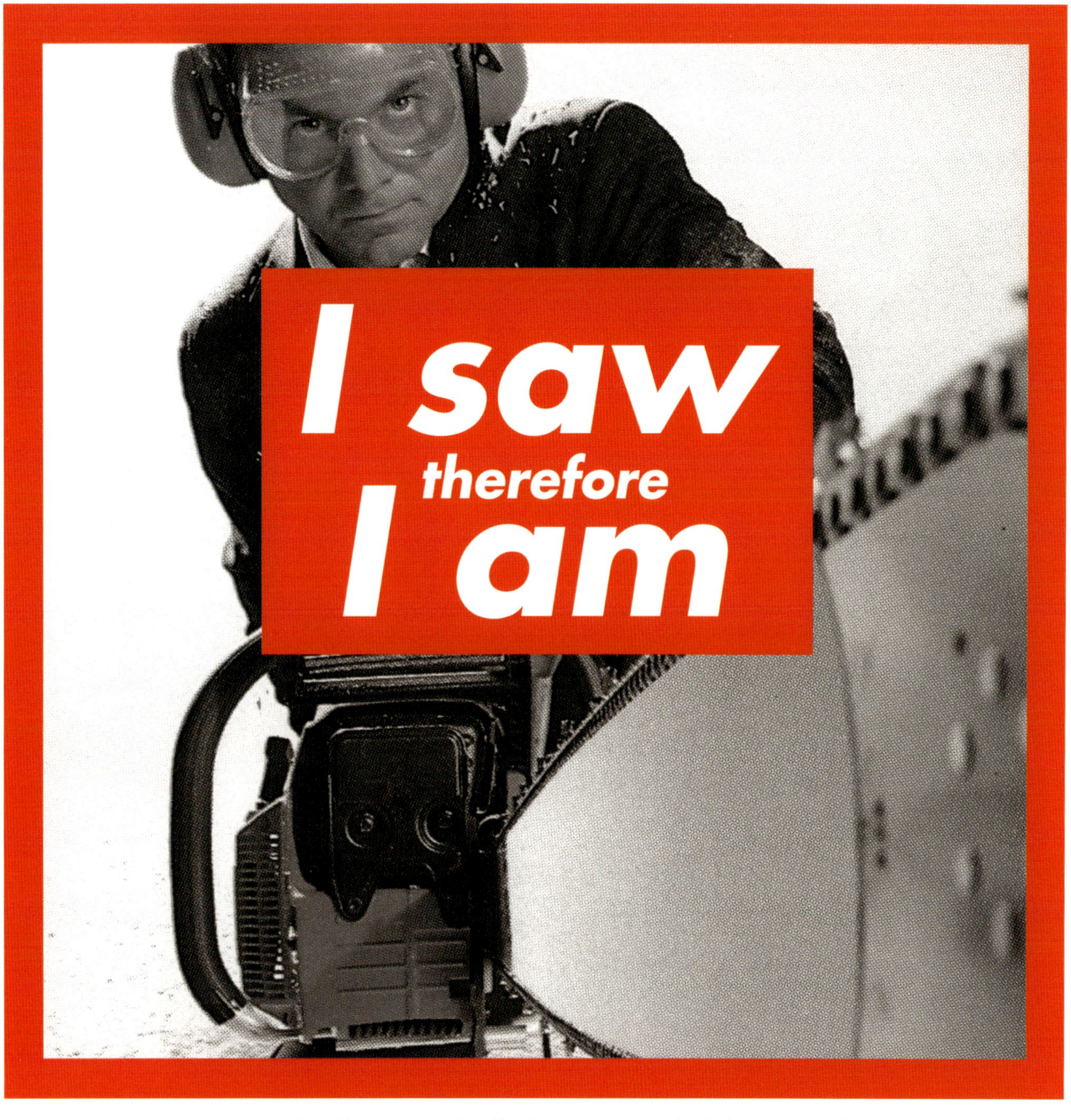

BARBARA KRUGER (b. 1945) American — ***I Saw Therefore I Am,*** 1987 — Archival inkjet print on vinyl — 55"x 55"

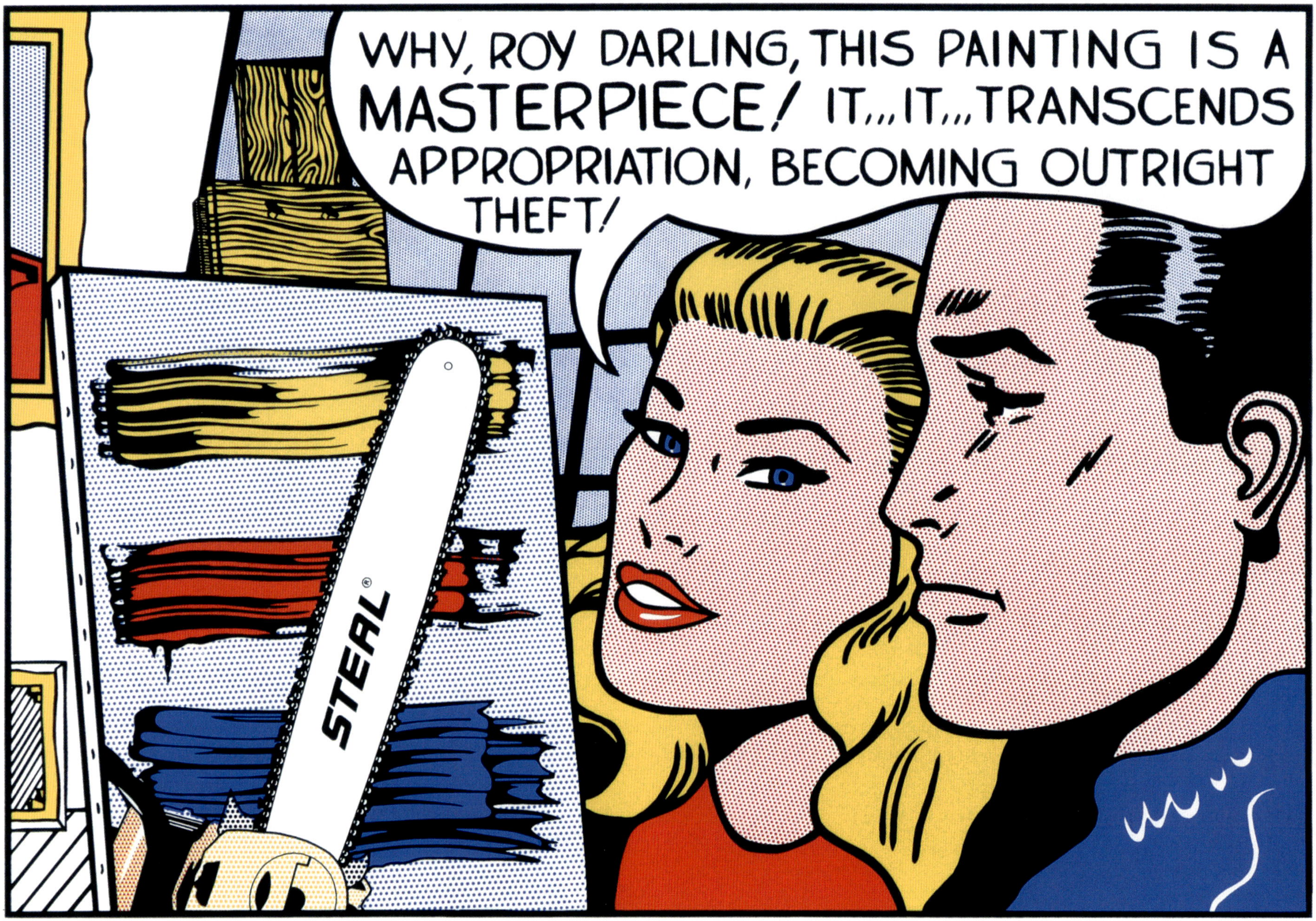

ROY LICHTENSTEIN (1923 - 1997) American — ***Why, Roy Darling,*** 1962 — Screenprint on paper — 30"x 40"

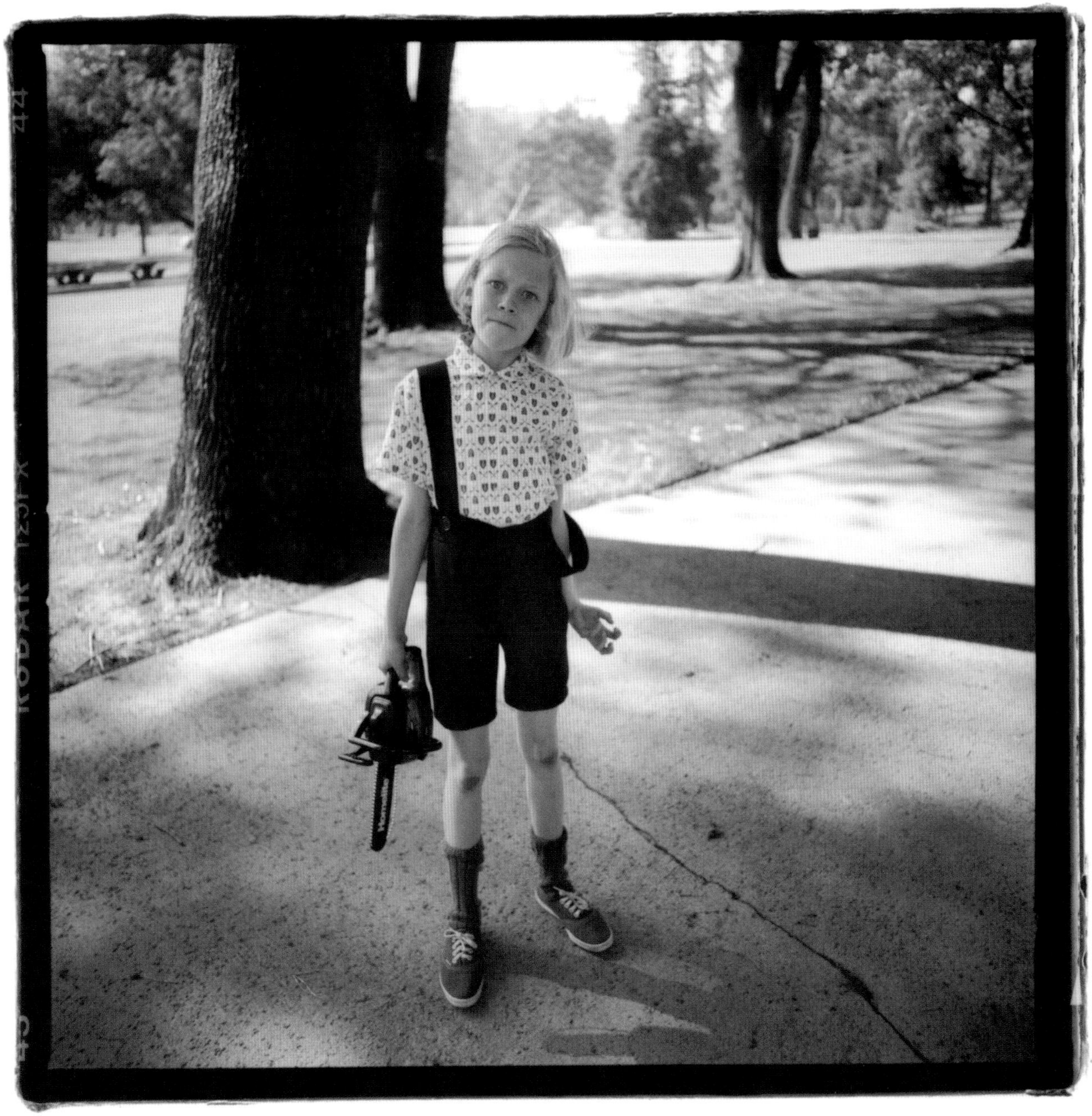

DIANE ARBUS (1923 - 1971) American — ***Child with toy chainsaw in Griffith Park,*** Los Angeles, 1962 — Gelatin silver print — 20"x 24"

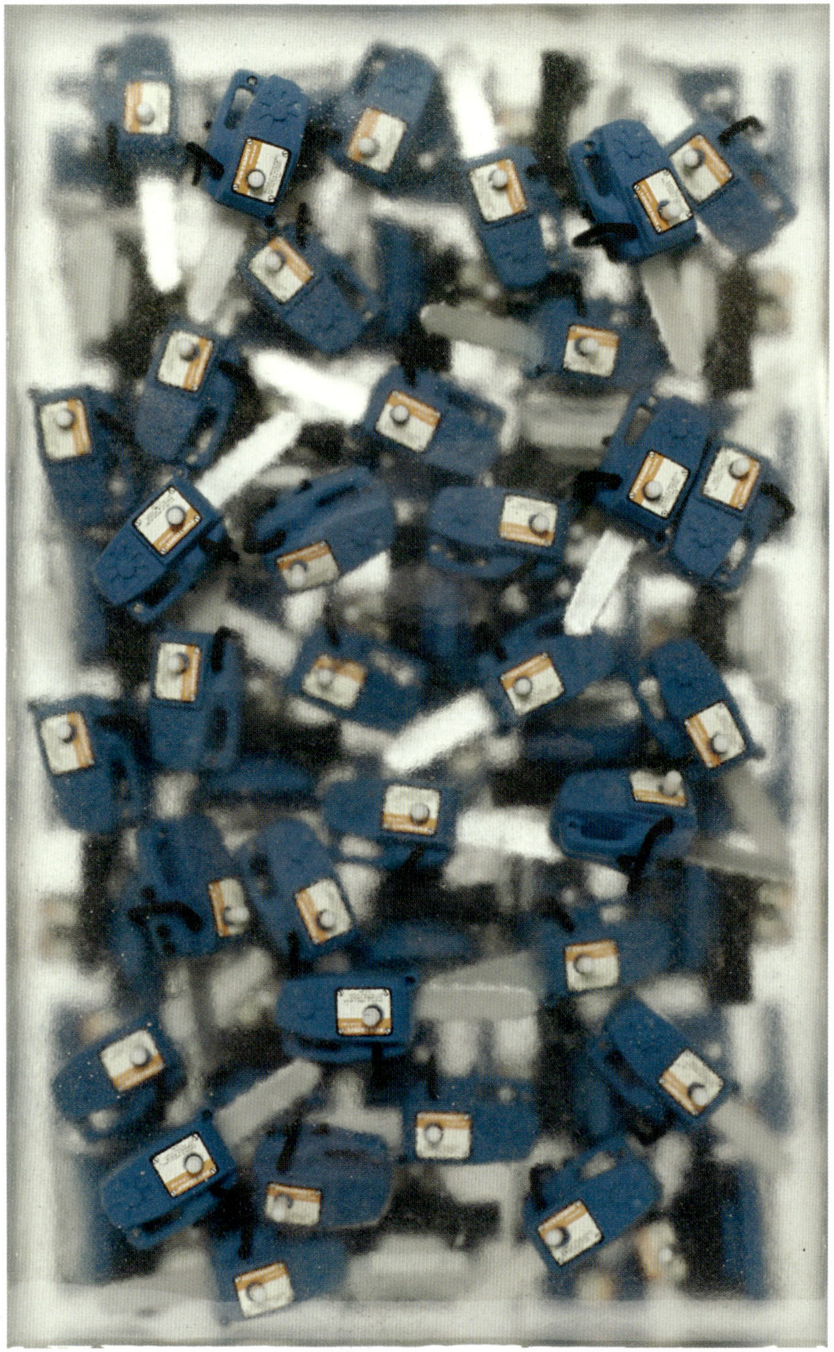

ARMAN (1928 - 2005) French — ***Accumulation of Chainsaws,*** 1980 — Plastic wind-up saws, resin — 10"x 16"x 3"

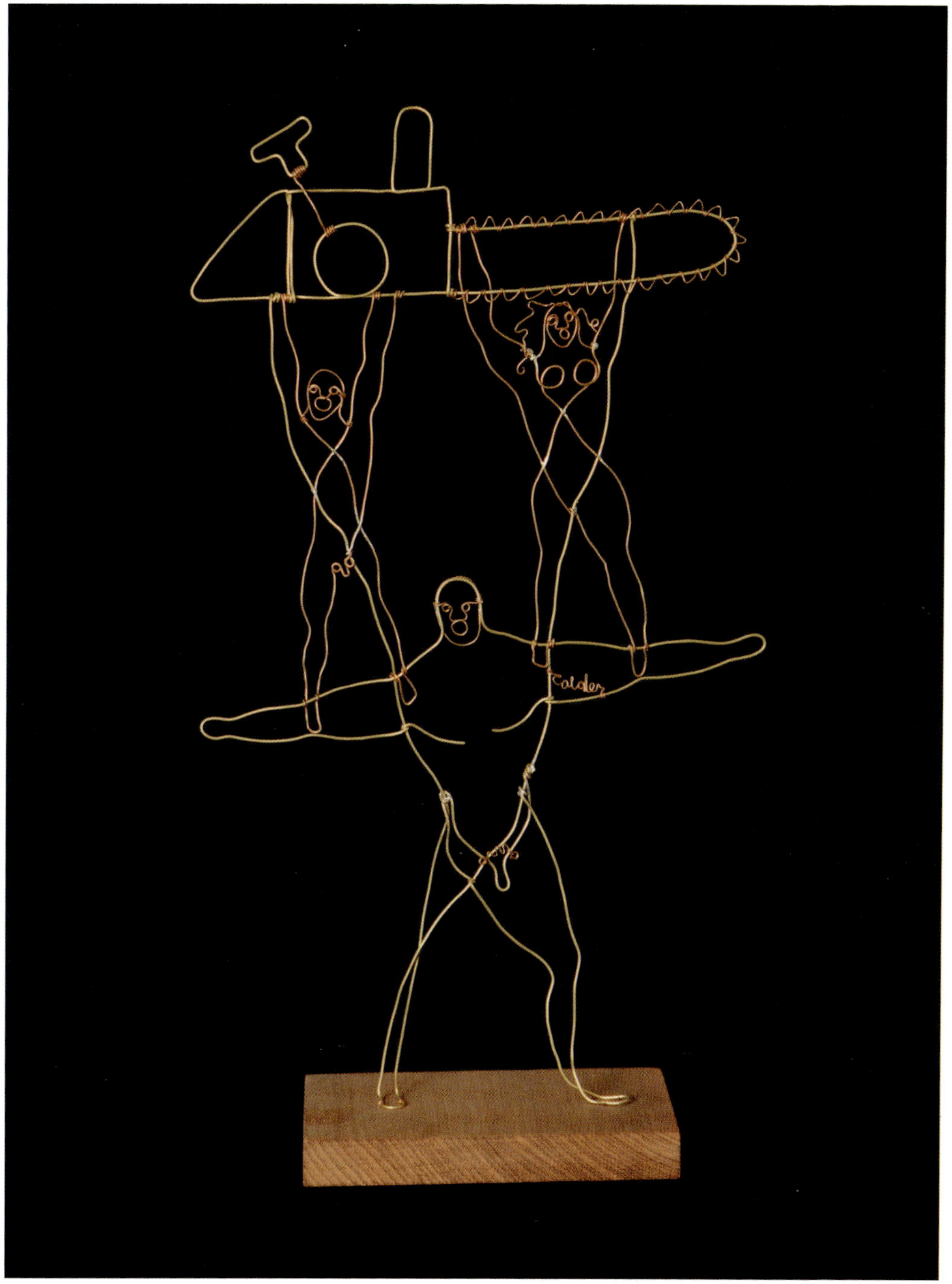

Calder (1898 - 1976) American — ***Three Acrobats, One Chainsaw,*** c.1928 — Wire and wood — 8"x 9"x 12"

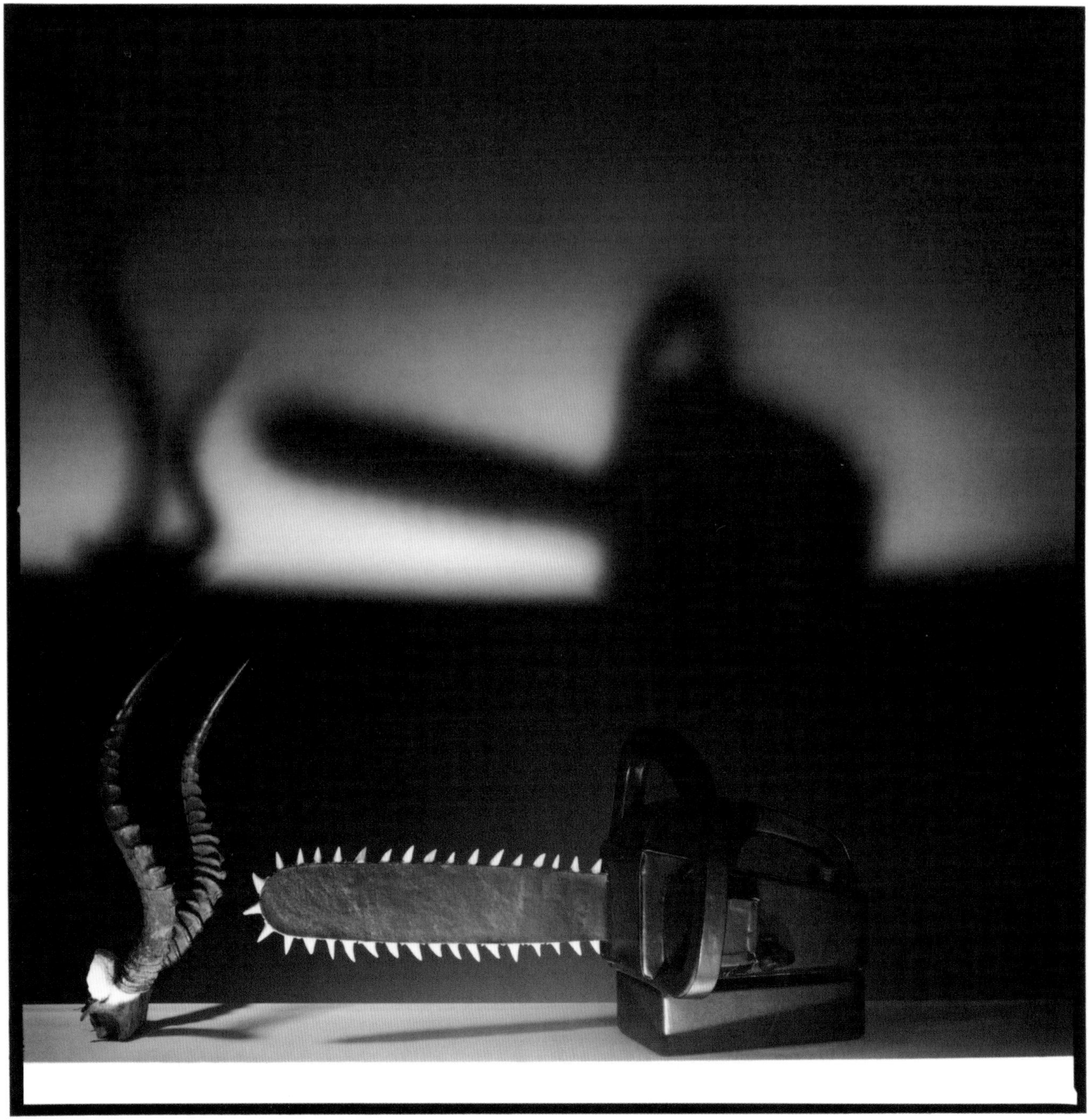

Robert Mapplethorpe (1946 - 1989) American — ***Grossman,*** 1985 — Gelatin silver print — 16"x 20"

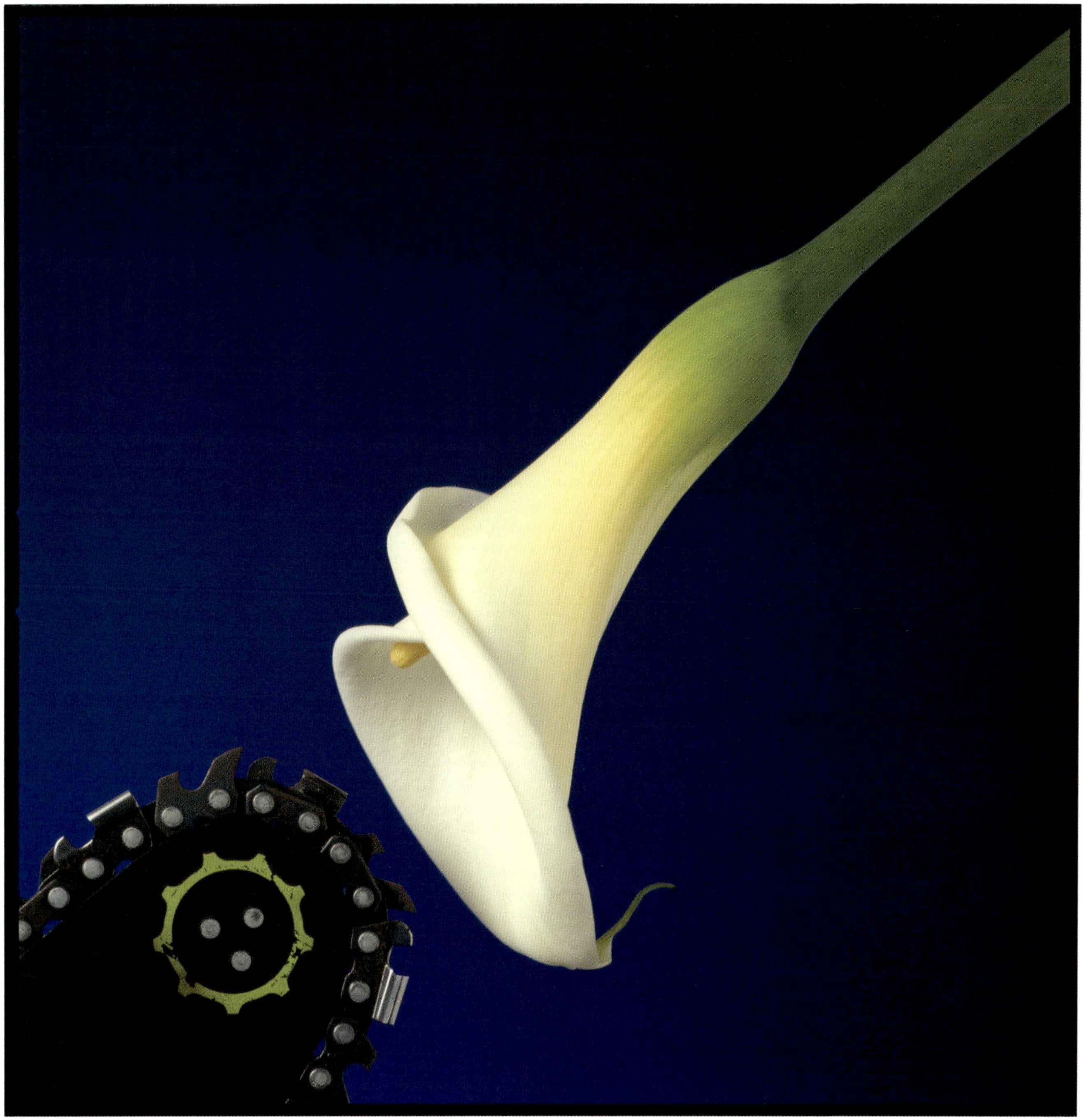

Robert Mapplethorpe (1946 - 1989) American — ***Calla Lily plus,*** 1986 — Digital type RA-4 print — 20"x 24"

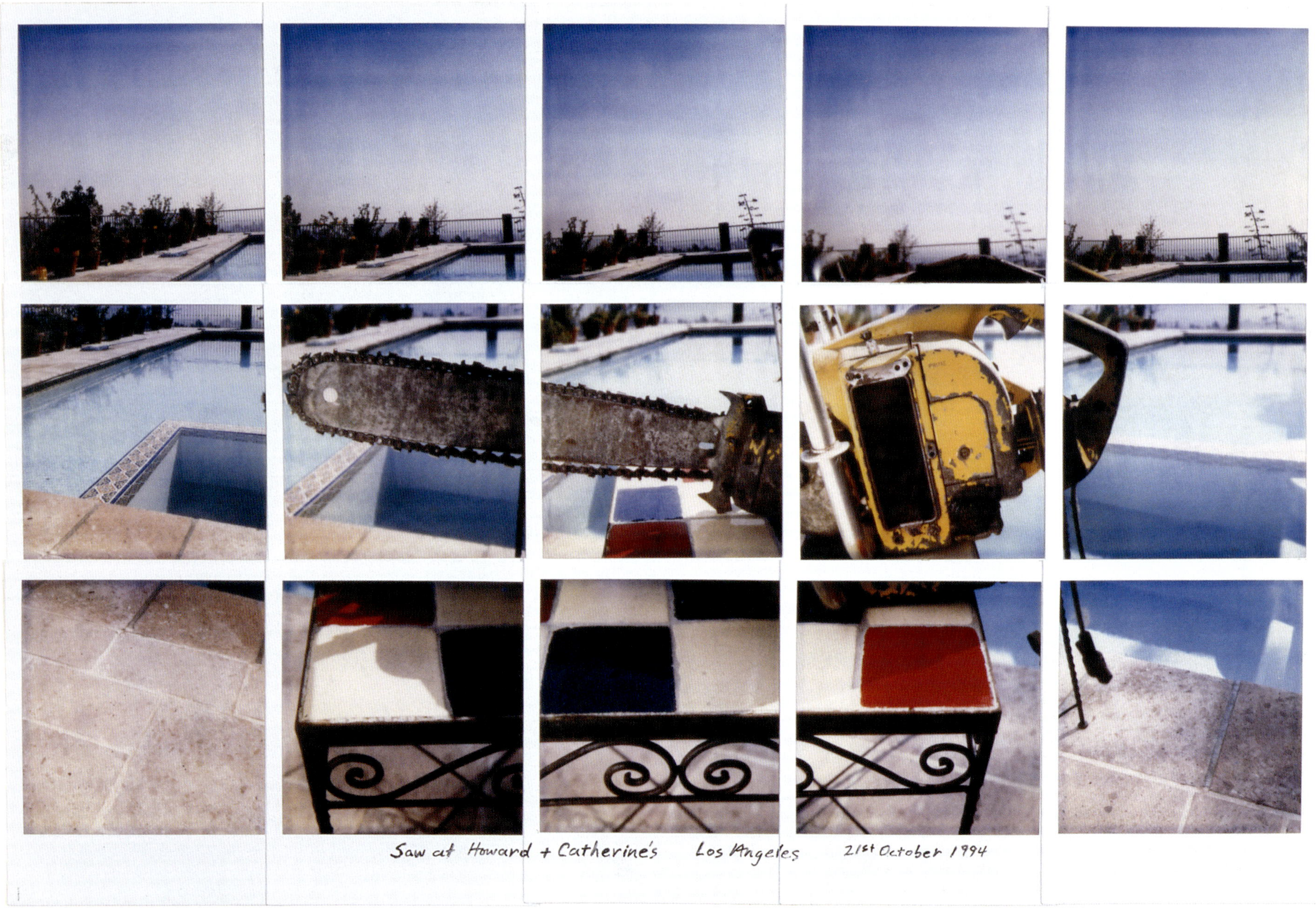

DAVID HOCKNEY (b. 1937) English — ***Saw at Howard and Catherine's****, 1994 — Polaroids on ragboard — 24"x 32"

*now ***Anne's***

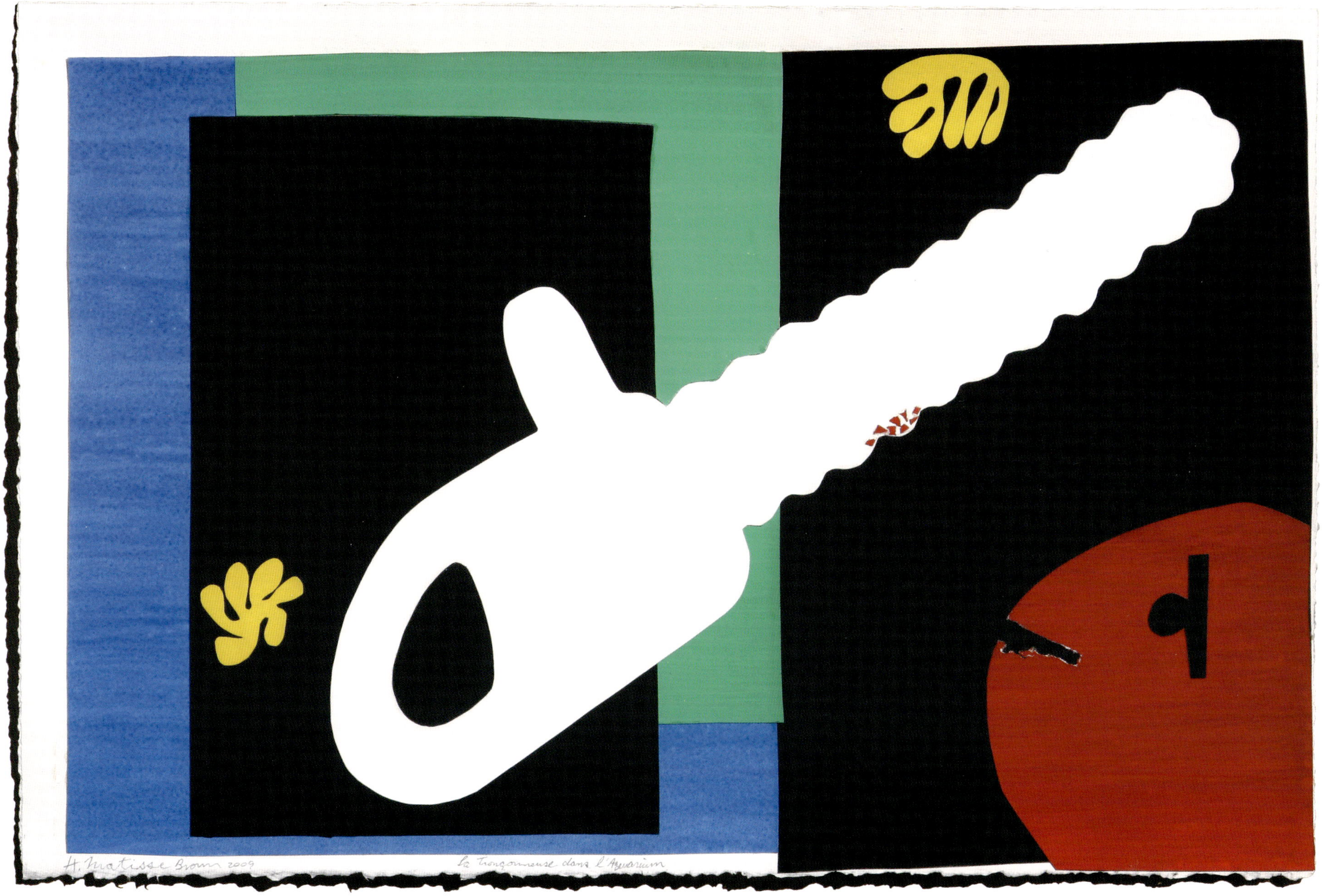

Henri Matisse (1869 - 1954) French — ***La Tronconneuse dans l'Aquarium,*** 1947 — Gouache on paper collage — 17"x 26"

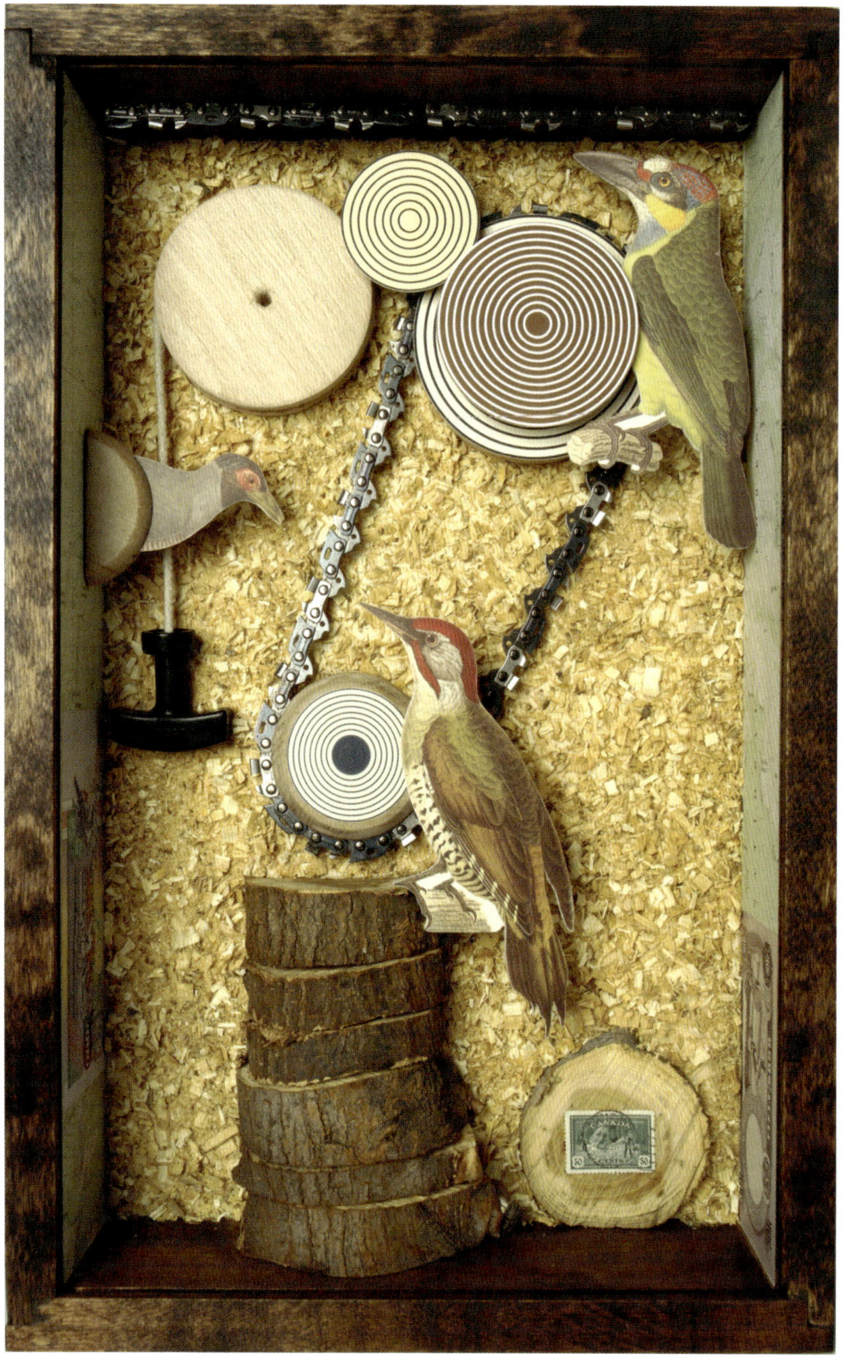

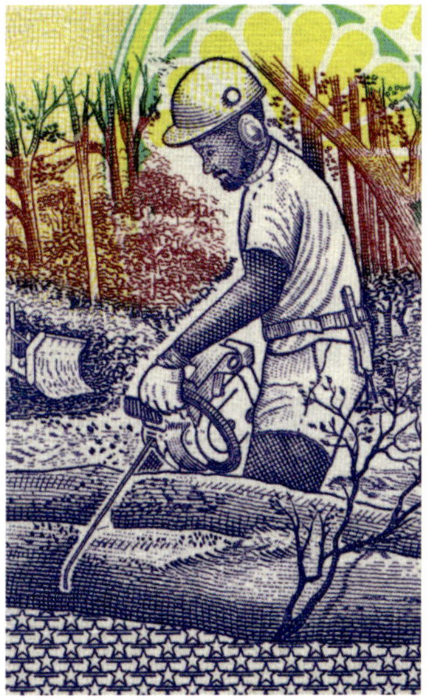

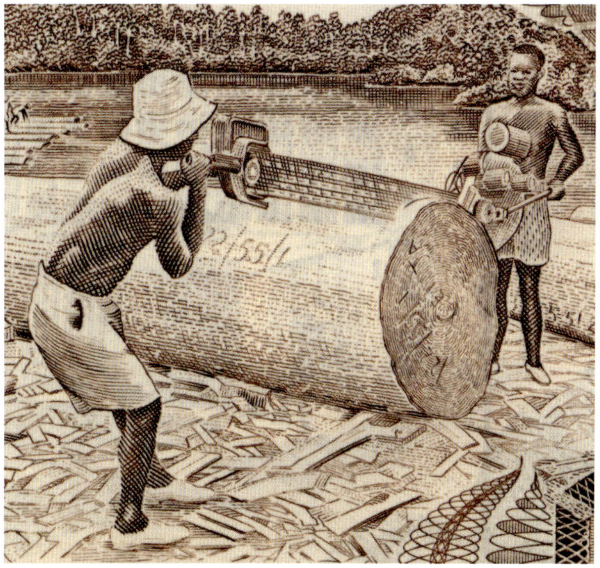

Facing page. JOSEPH CORNELL (1903 - 1972) American — ***Untitled (Woodpecker Habitat),*** 1946 — Various woods, engravings, chainsaw chain, map, stamps, currency, rubber handle, rope

JOSEPH CORNELL (1903 - 1972) American — Detail of stamps in ***Untitled (Woodpecker Habitat),*** 1946

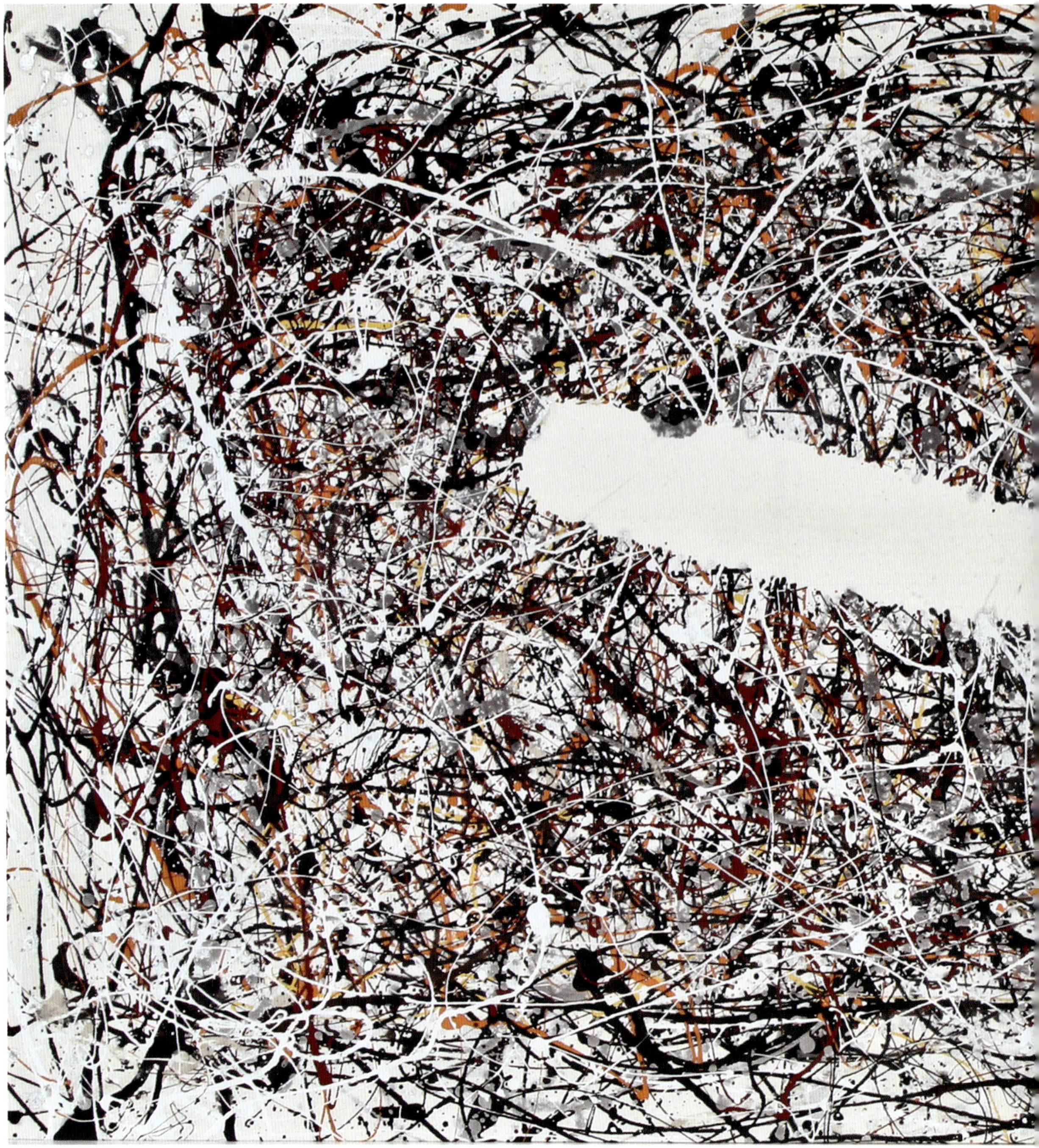

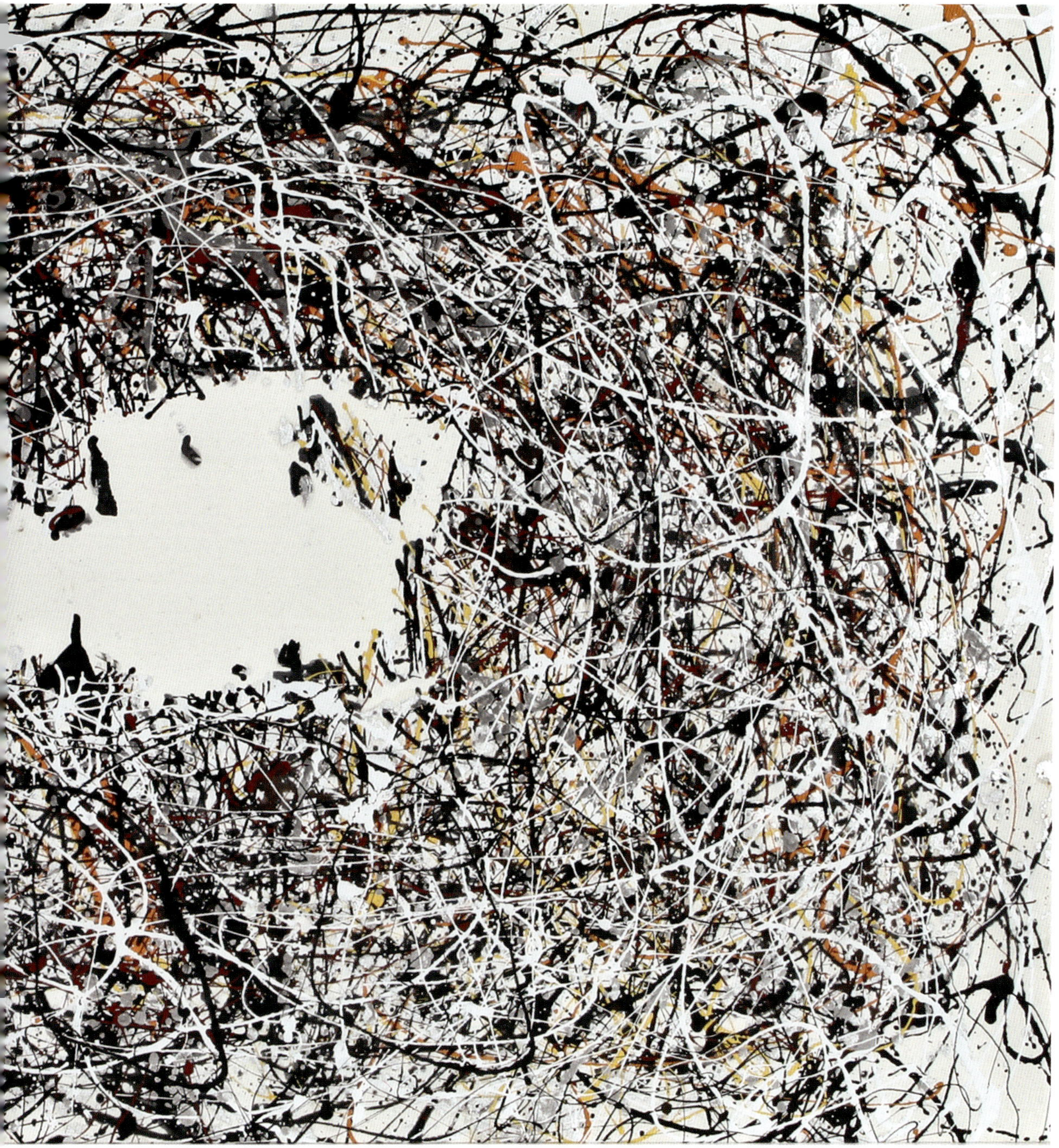

JACKSON POLLOCK (1912 - 1956) American — ***Arterial Mist,*** 1950 — Enamel, aluminum paint and oil on canvas — 40"x 78"

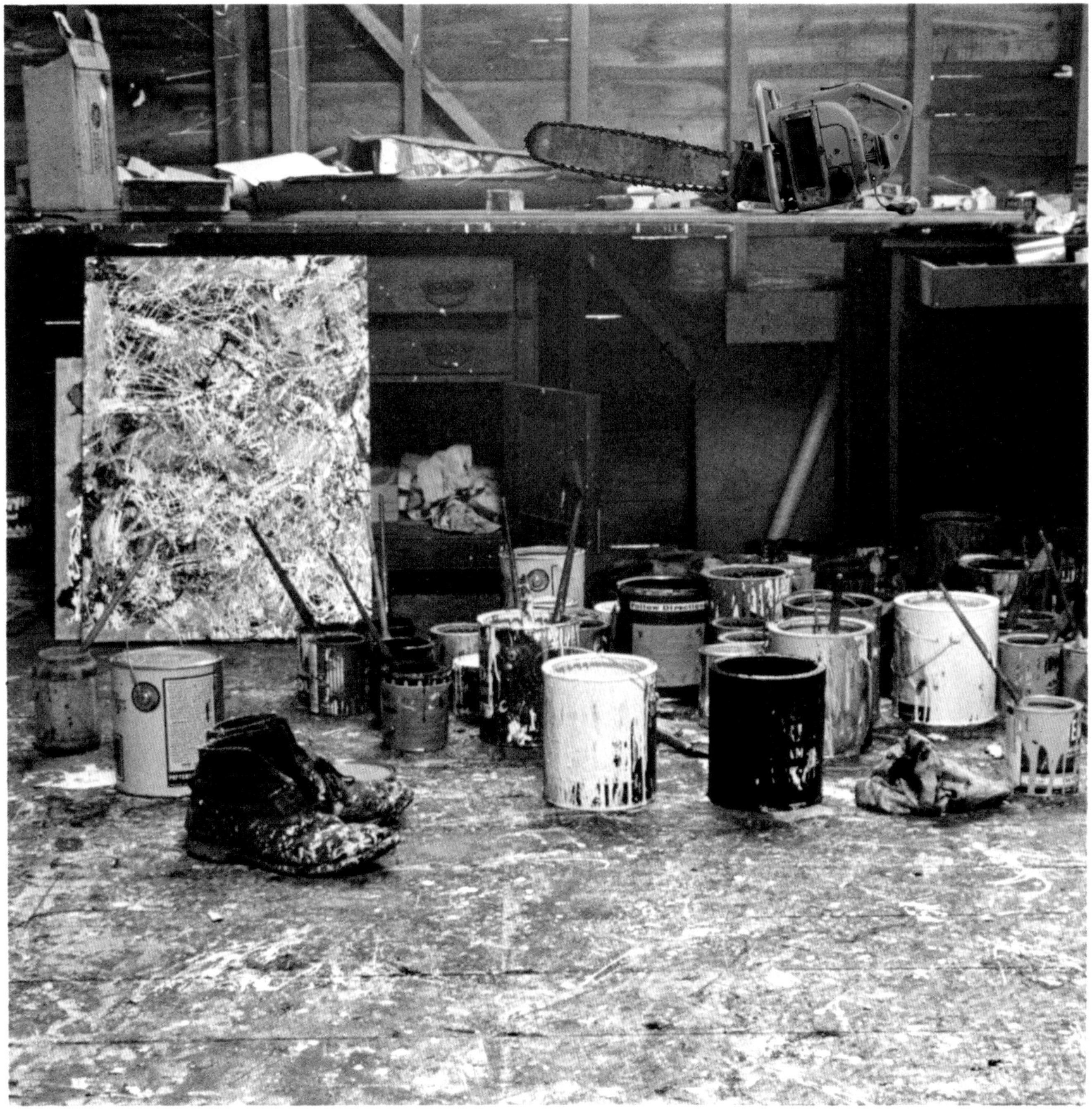

HANS NAMUTH (1915 - 1990) German — ***Pollock's Studio, Before,*** 1950 — Digital type RA-4 print — 8"x 10"

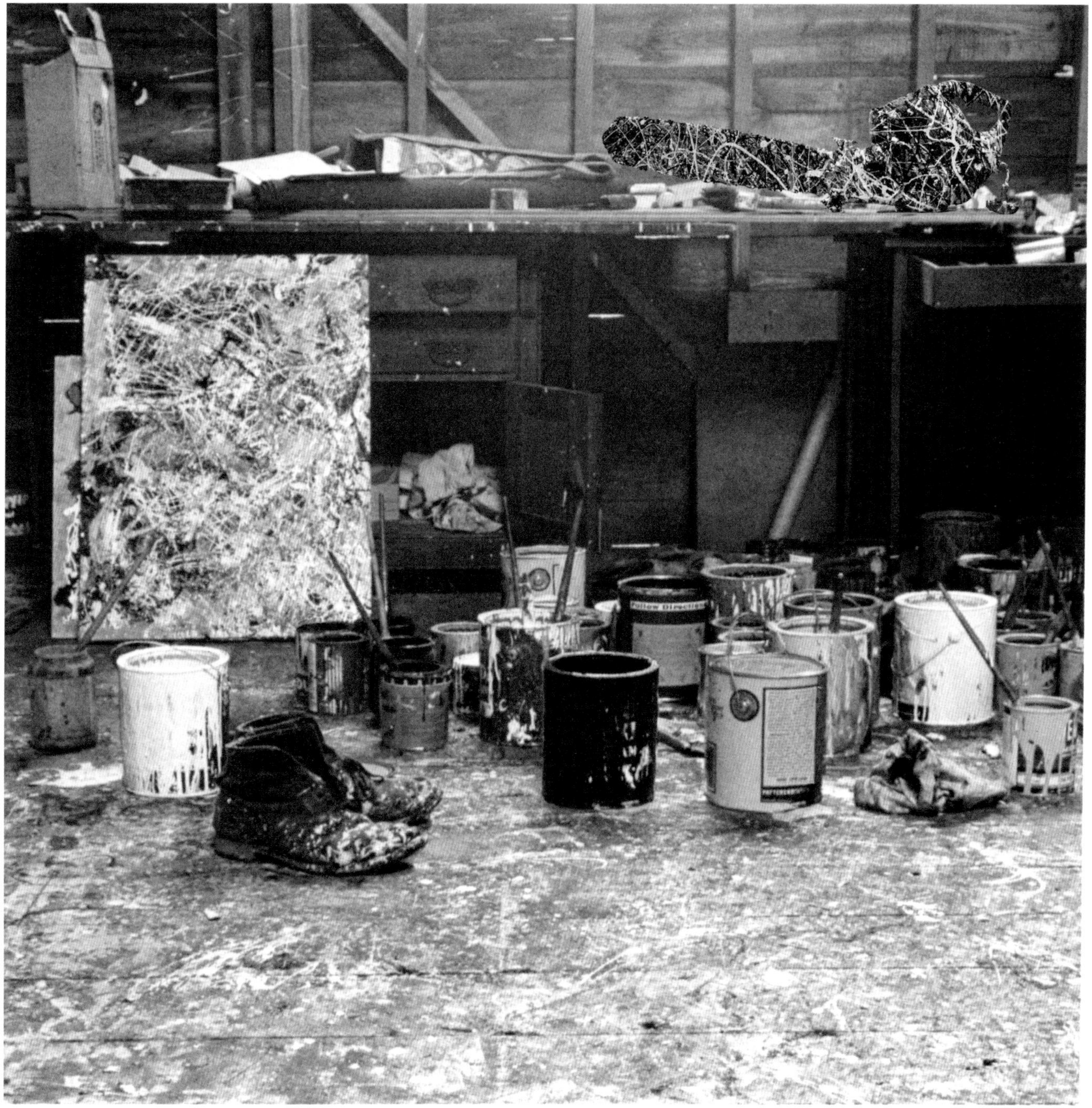

Hans Namuth (1915 - 1990) German — ***Pollock's Studio, After,*** 1950 — Digital type RA-4 print — 8"x 10"

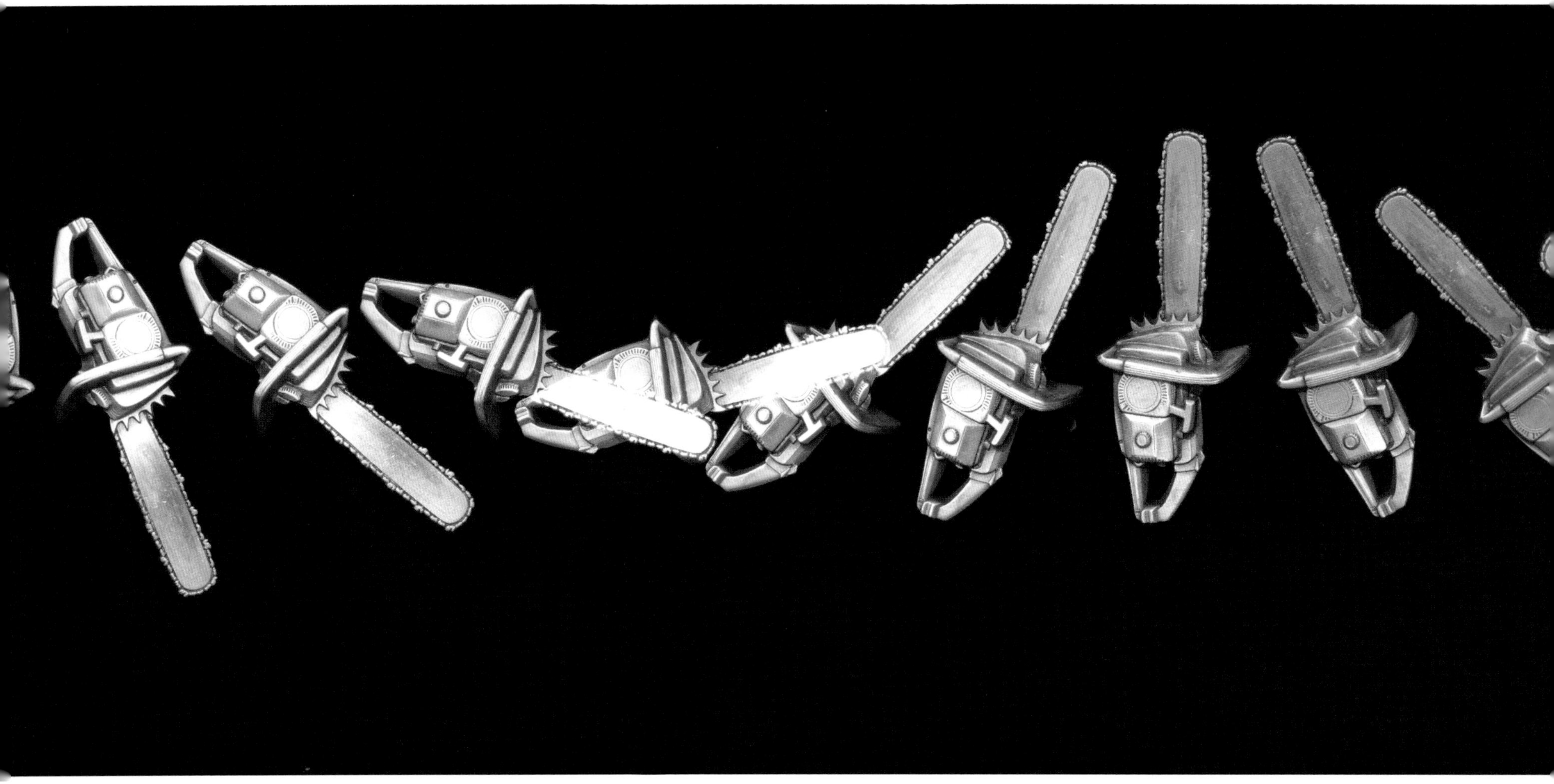

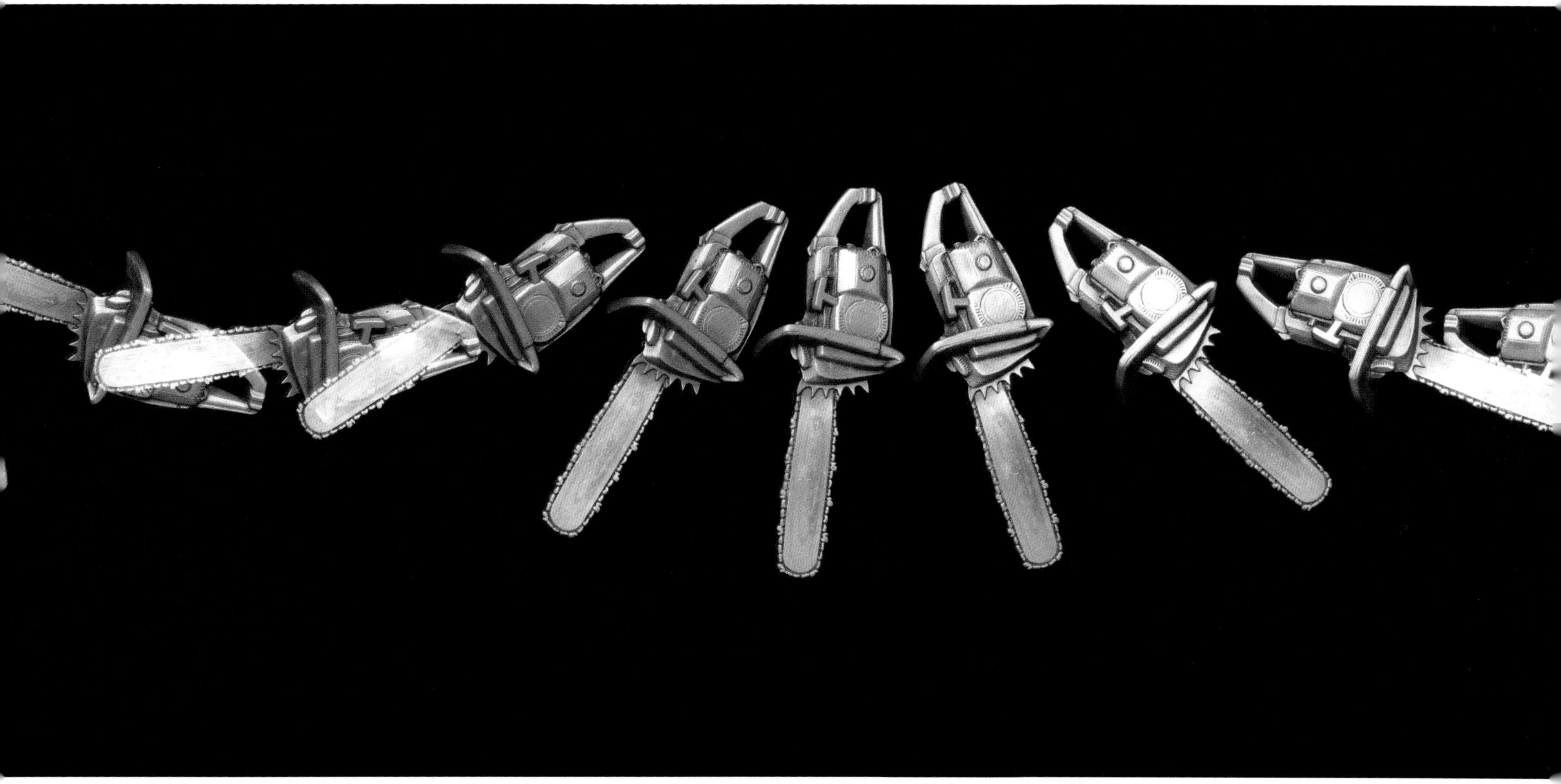

Berenice Abbott (1898 - 1991) American — ***Spinning Chainsaw,*** 1958 — Digital type RA-4 print — 12"x 40"

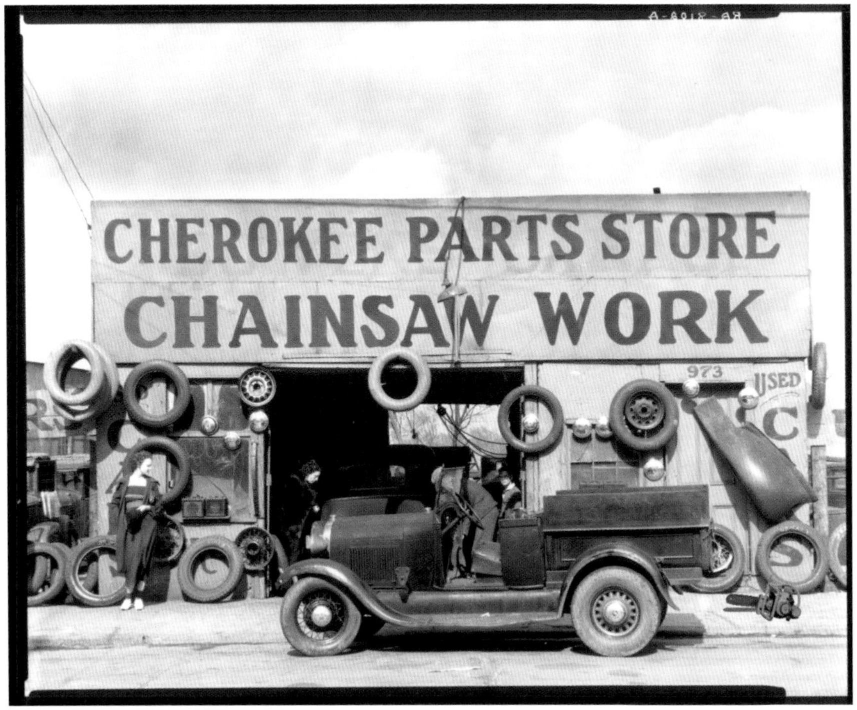

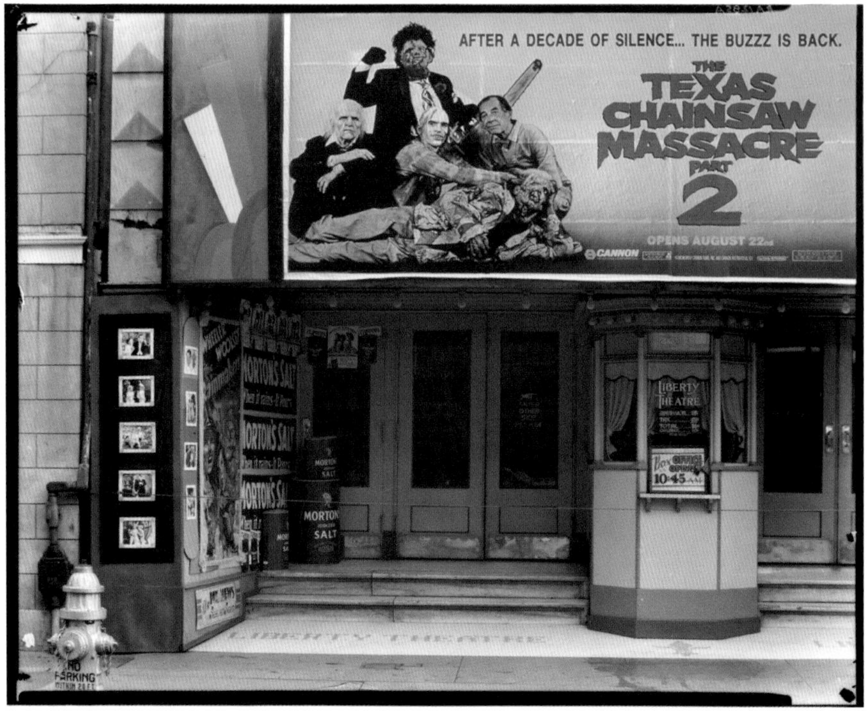

Left. WALKER EVANS (1903 - 1975) American — ***Chainsaw parts shop. Atlanta, Georgia,*** 1936 — Archival inkjet print on paper — 8"x 10"

Right. WALKER EVANS (1903 - 1975) American — ***Movie theatre on Saint Charles Street. Liberty Theater, New Orleans, Louisiana,*** 1936 (?) — Archival inkjet print on paper — 8"x 10"

Facing page. WALKER EVANS (1903 - 1975) American — ***General store interior. Moundville, Alabama,*** 1936 — Archival inkjet print on paper — 8"x 10"

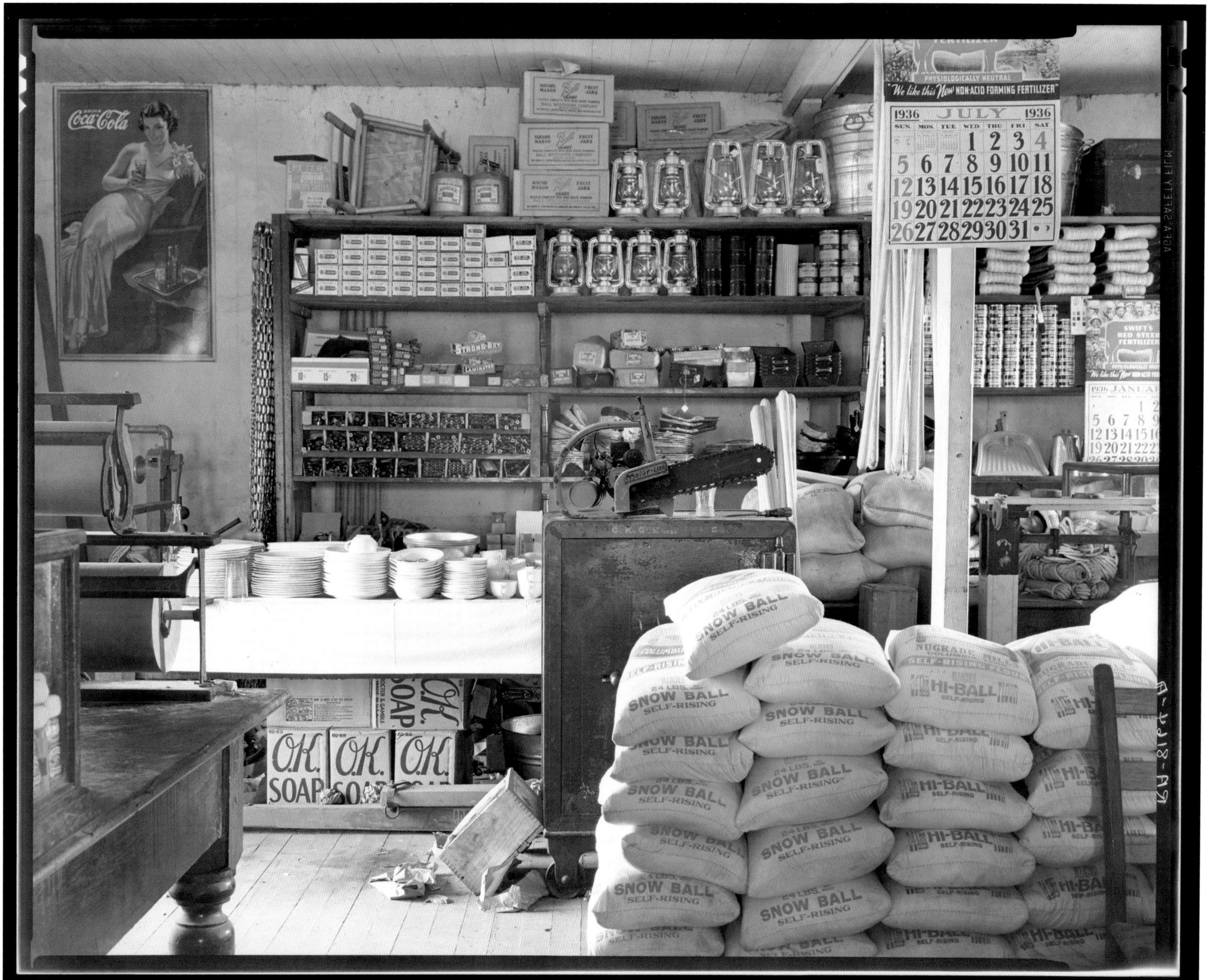

Coca-Cola
PHYSIOLOGICALLY NEUTRAL
"We like this New NON-ACID FORMING FERTILIZER"
1936 JULY 1936
SUN. MON. TUE. WED. THU. FRI. SAT.
1 2 3 4
5 6 7 8 9 10 11
12 13 14 15 16 17 18
19 20 21 22 23 24 25
26 27 28 29 30 31
FRUIT JARS
STRONG-BOY
O.K. SOAP
SNOW BALL SELF-RISING
24 LBS.
HI-BALL SELF-RISING
NUGRADE

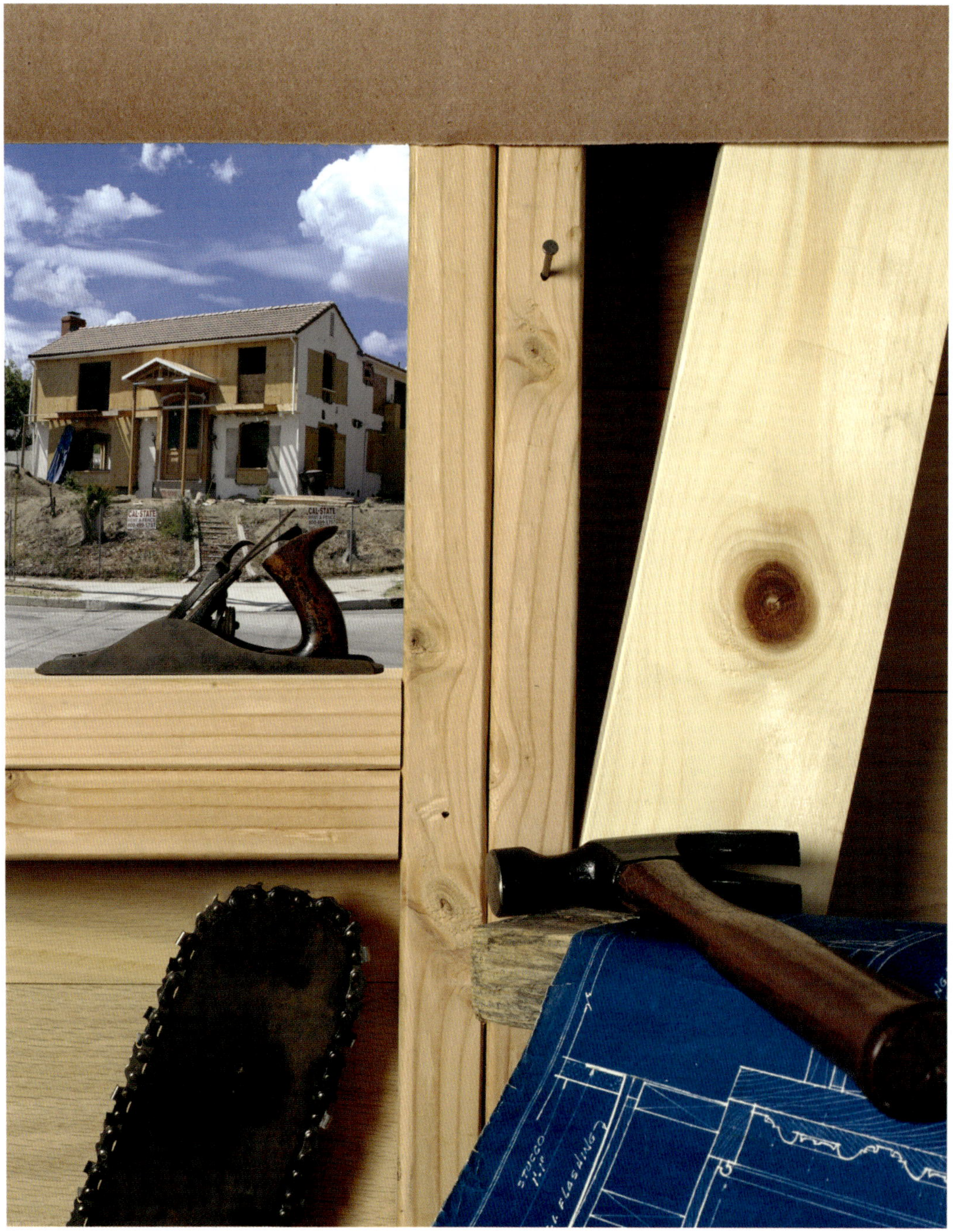

PAUL OUTERBRIDGE (1896 - 1958) American — ***Tools with Blueprint,*** 1939 — Digital type RA-4 print — 13"x 17"

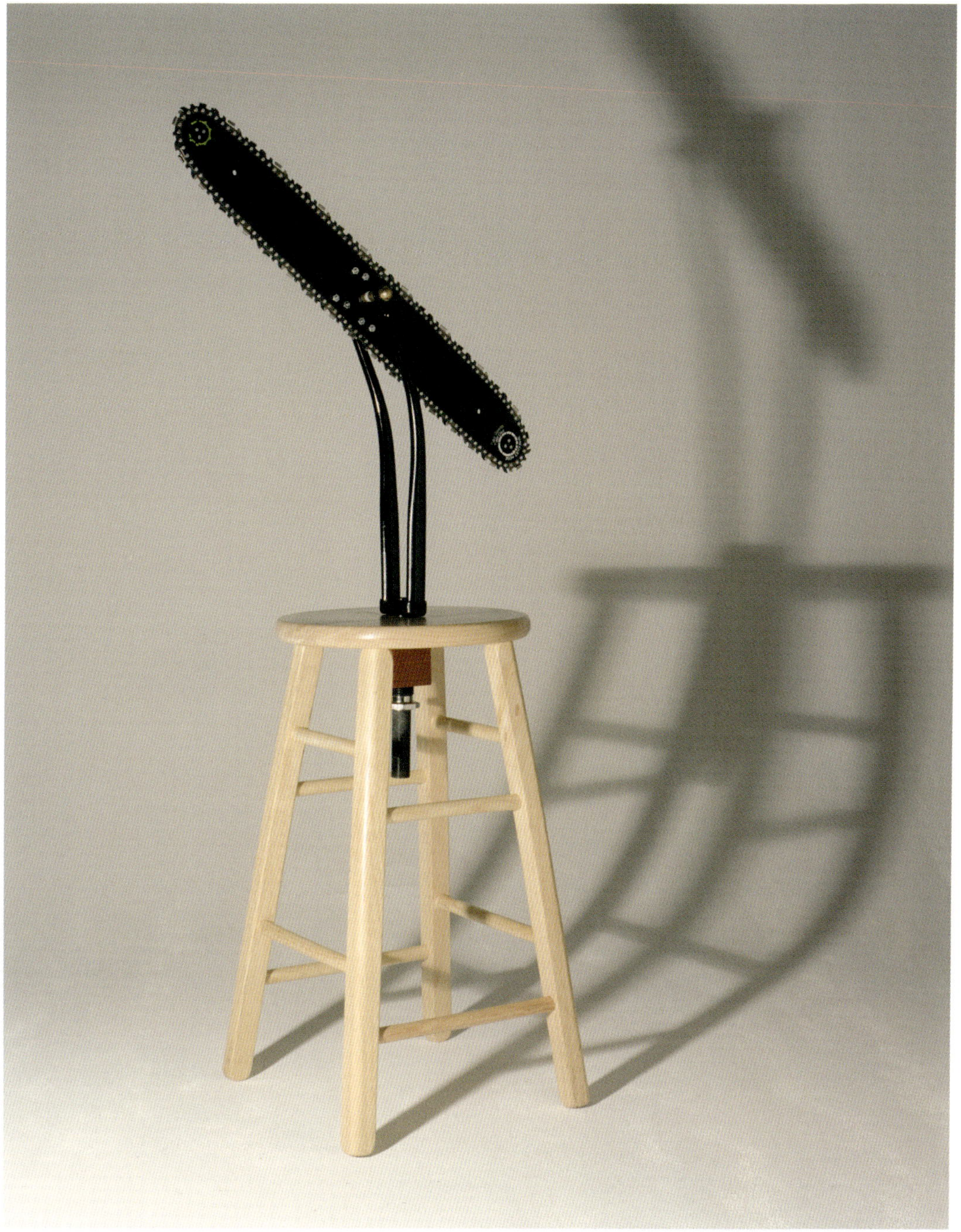

MARCEL DUCHAMP (1887 - 1968) French — ***Bicycle Bar,*** 1951 (third version, after lost original of 1913) — Wood stool, bicycle fork, chainsaw bars and chain, Padouk wood — 16"x 16"x 60"

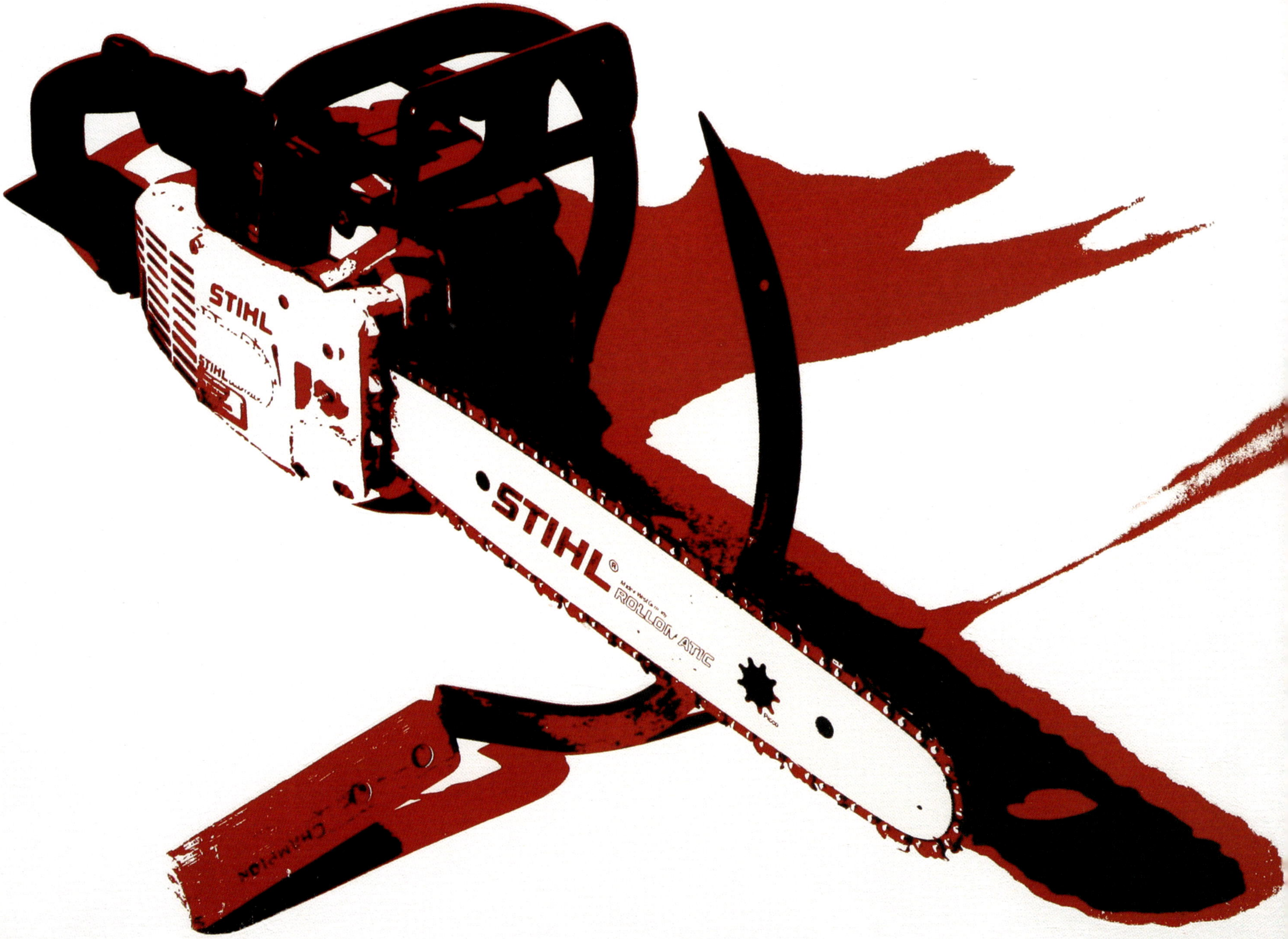
STIHL
STIHL®
ROLLOMATIC

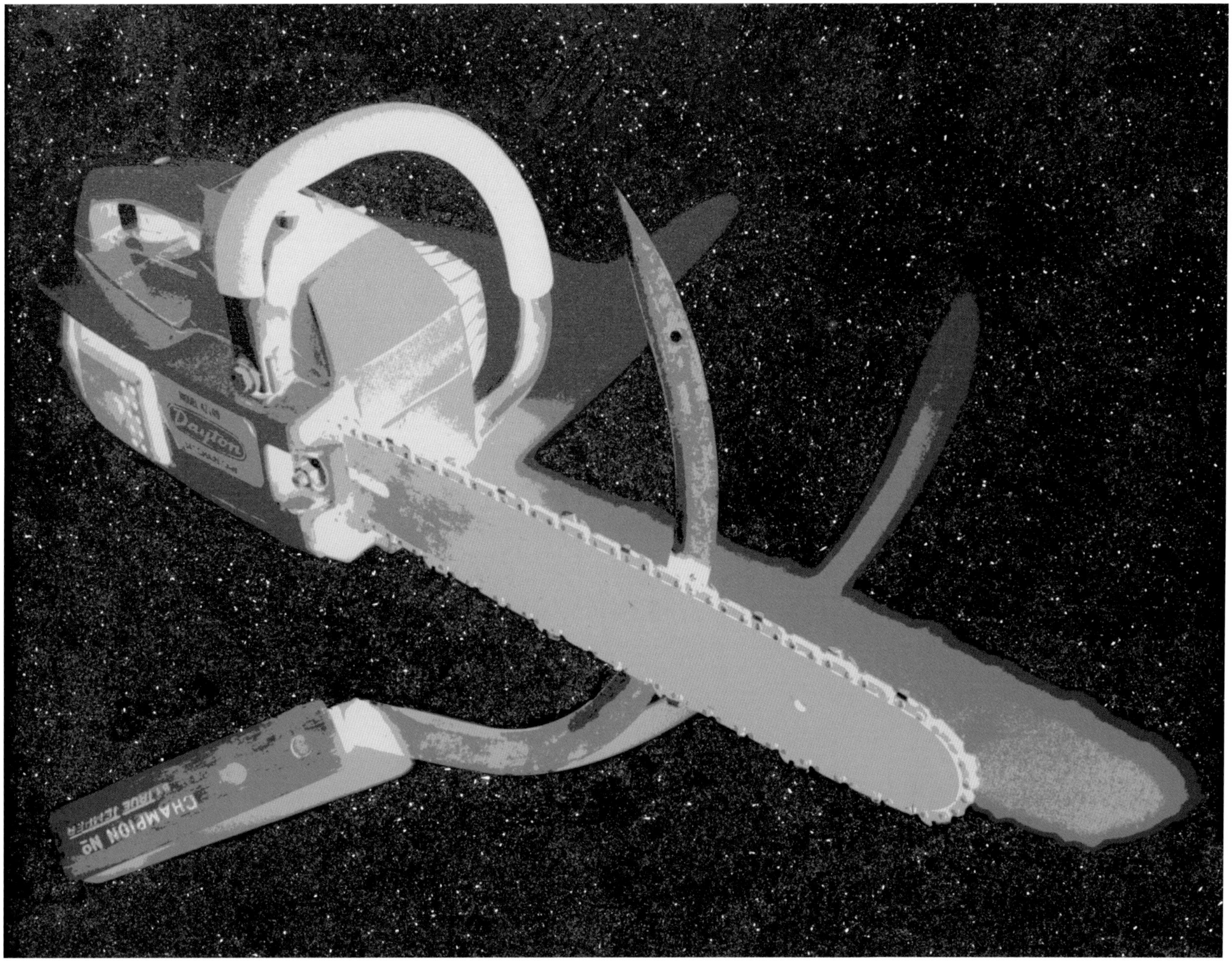

Facing page. ANDY WARHOL (1928 - 1987) American — ***Chainsaw and Sickle,*** 1976 — Screenprint and acrylic on canvas — 24"x 30"

ANDY WARHOL (1928 - 1987) American — ***Diamond Dust Chainsaw and Sickle,*** 1976 — Archival inkjet, diamond dust and acrylic on canvas — 24"x30"

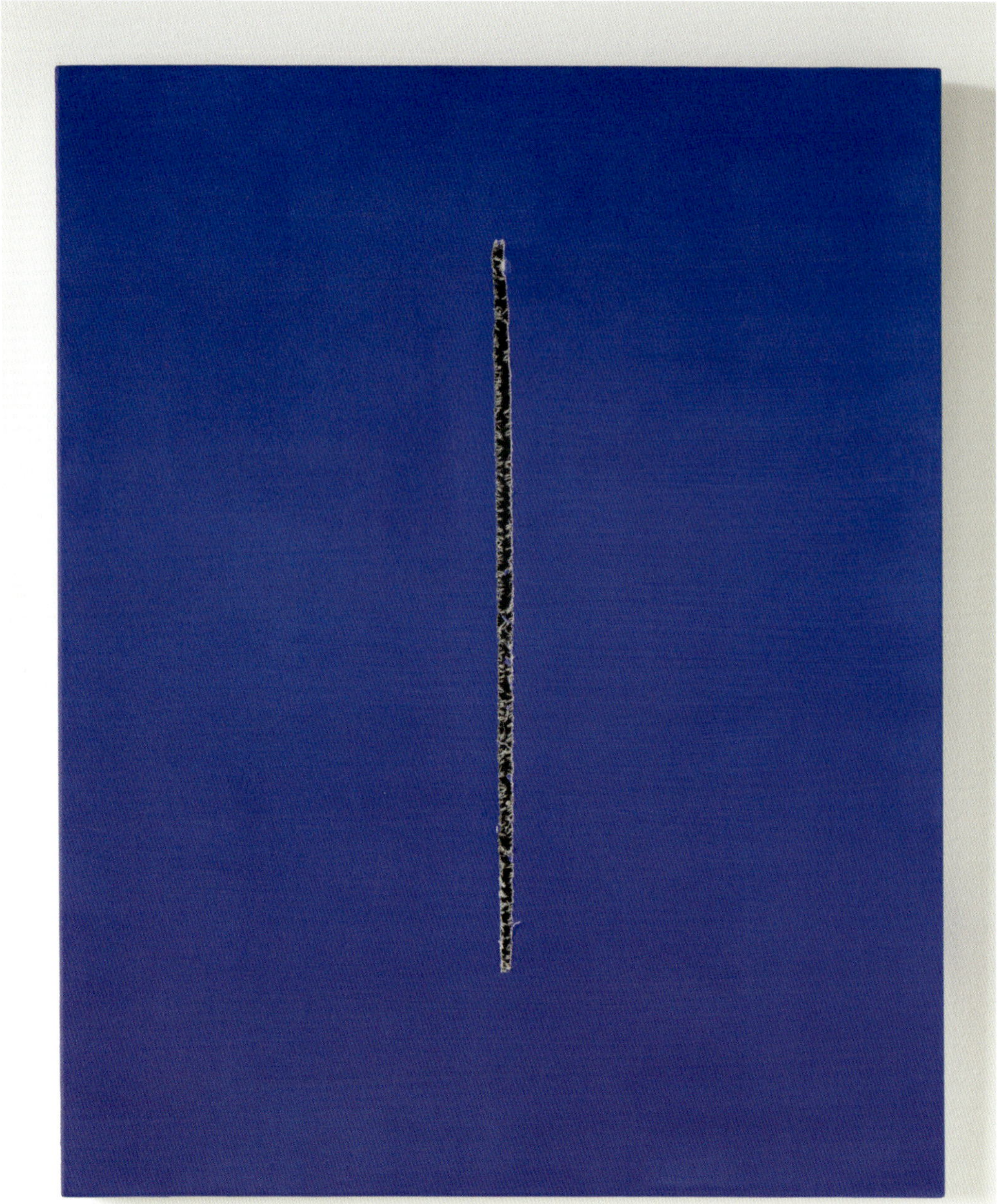

LUCIO FONTANA (1898 - 1968) Italian — ***Concetto spaziale, Attesa,*** 1965 — Waterpaint and chainsaw lubricating oil on canvas — 24"x 30"

Facing page. ED RUSCHA (b. 1937) American — ***Another one of them bikini and chainsaw movies,*** 2000 — Screenprint on paper — 28"x 34"

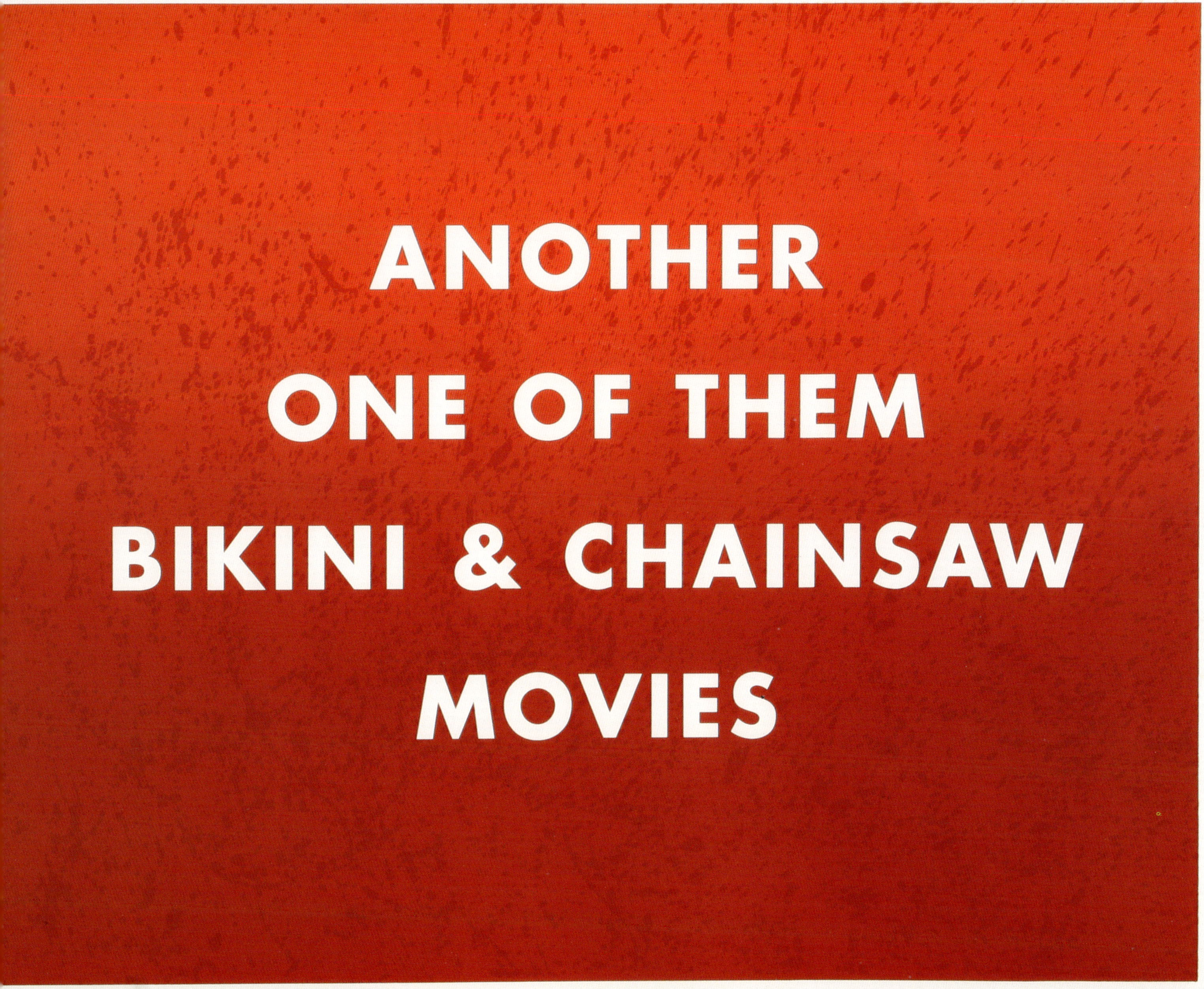
ANOTHER
ONE OF THEM
BIKINI & CHAINSAW
MOVIES

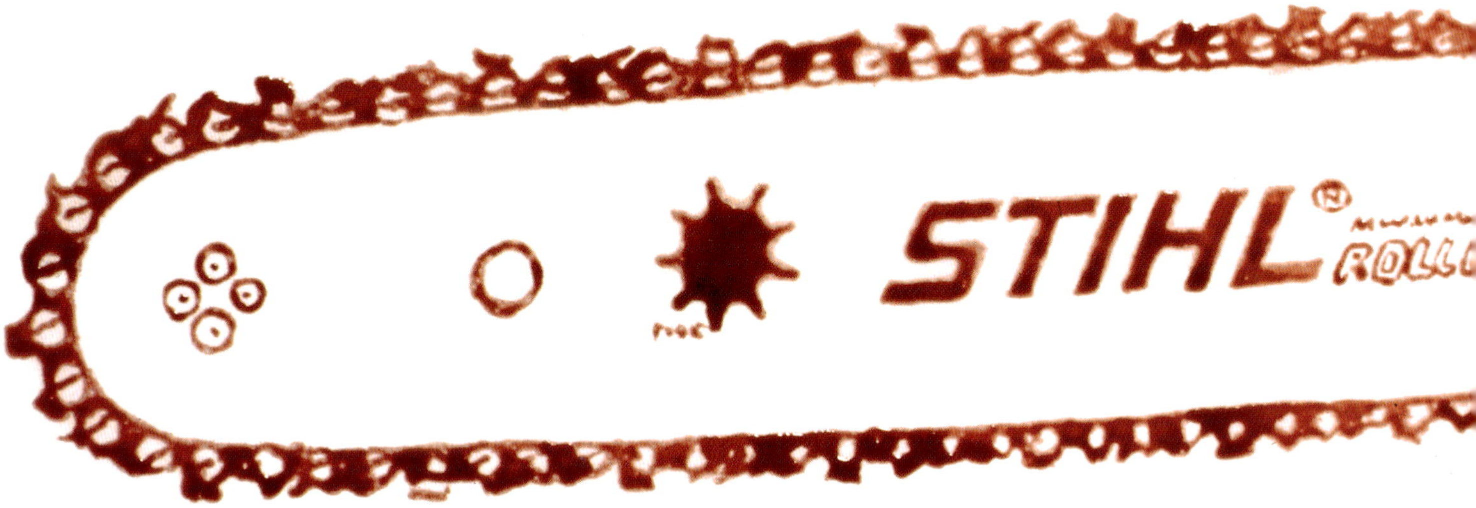

VIK MUNIZ (b. 1961) Brazilian — ***Chainsaw, from "Pictures of Stage Blood,"*** 2003 — Digital type RA-4 print — 16"x 20"

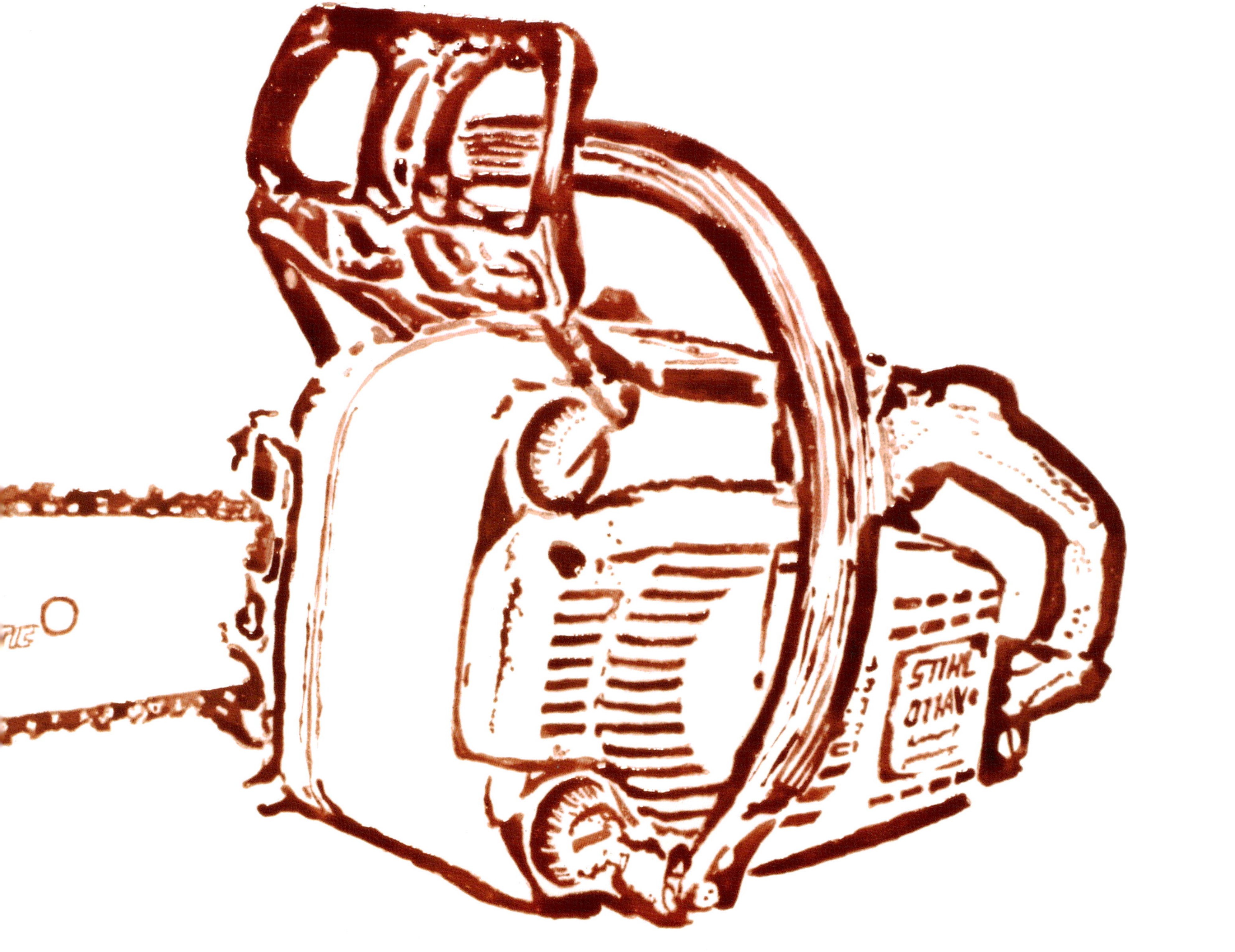
STIHL

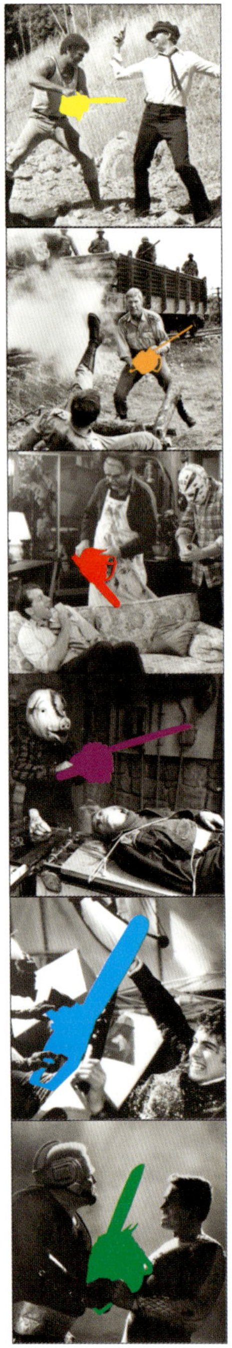

JOHN BALDESSARI (b. 1931) American — ***Chainsaw Fighting (from Yellow to Green)***, 2004 — Digital archival inkjet prints — 16"x 96"

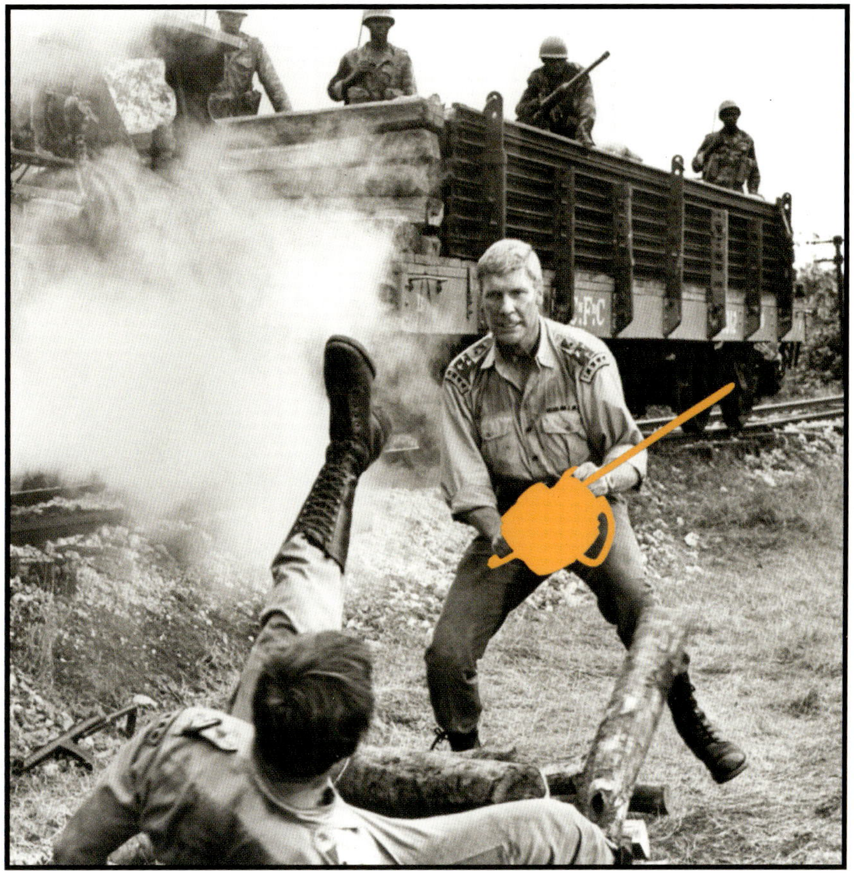

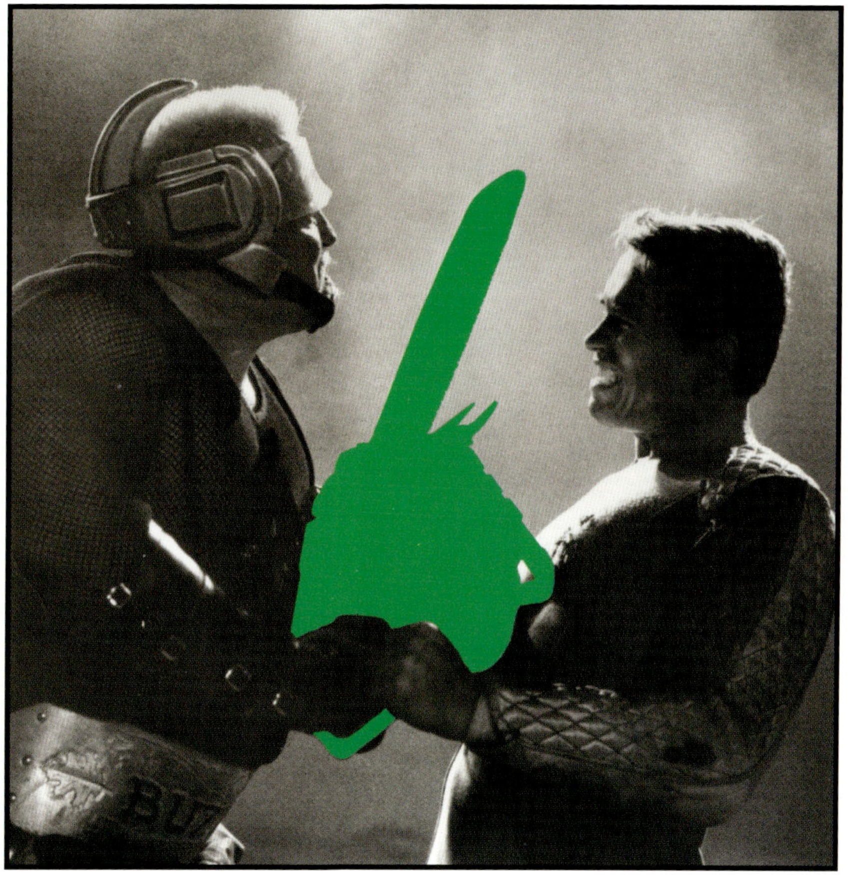
BUZ

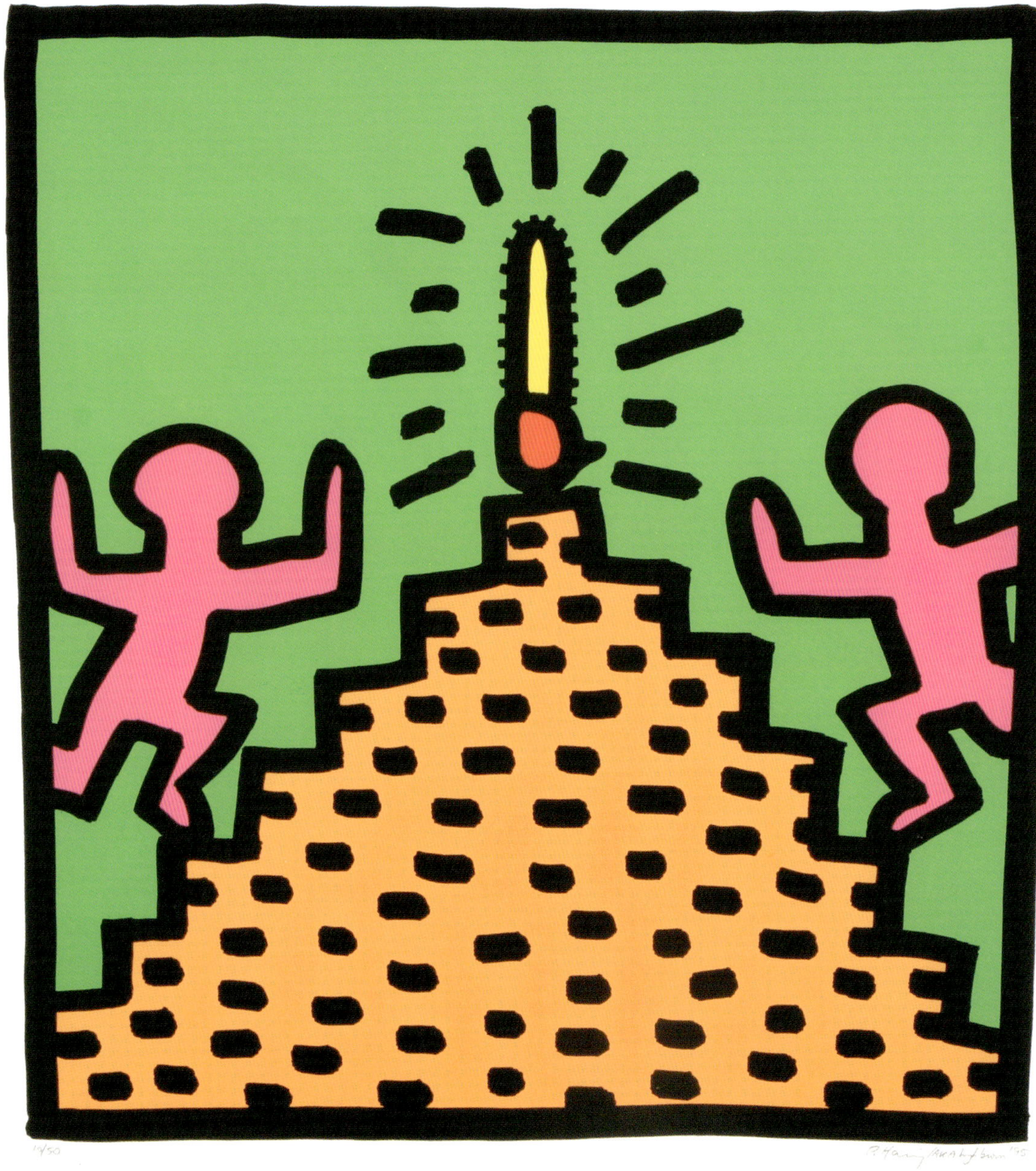

KEITH HARING (1958 - 1990) American — ***Untitled***, 1995 — Screenprint on paper — 22"x 24"

Facing page. MERET OPPENHEIM (1913-1985) German-born Swiss — ***Object (La tronconneuse en fourrure)***, 1936 — Plastic chainsaw, faux Chinese antelope fur, platter — 19"x 12"x 9 ½"

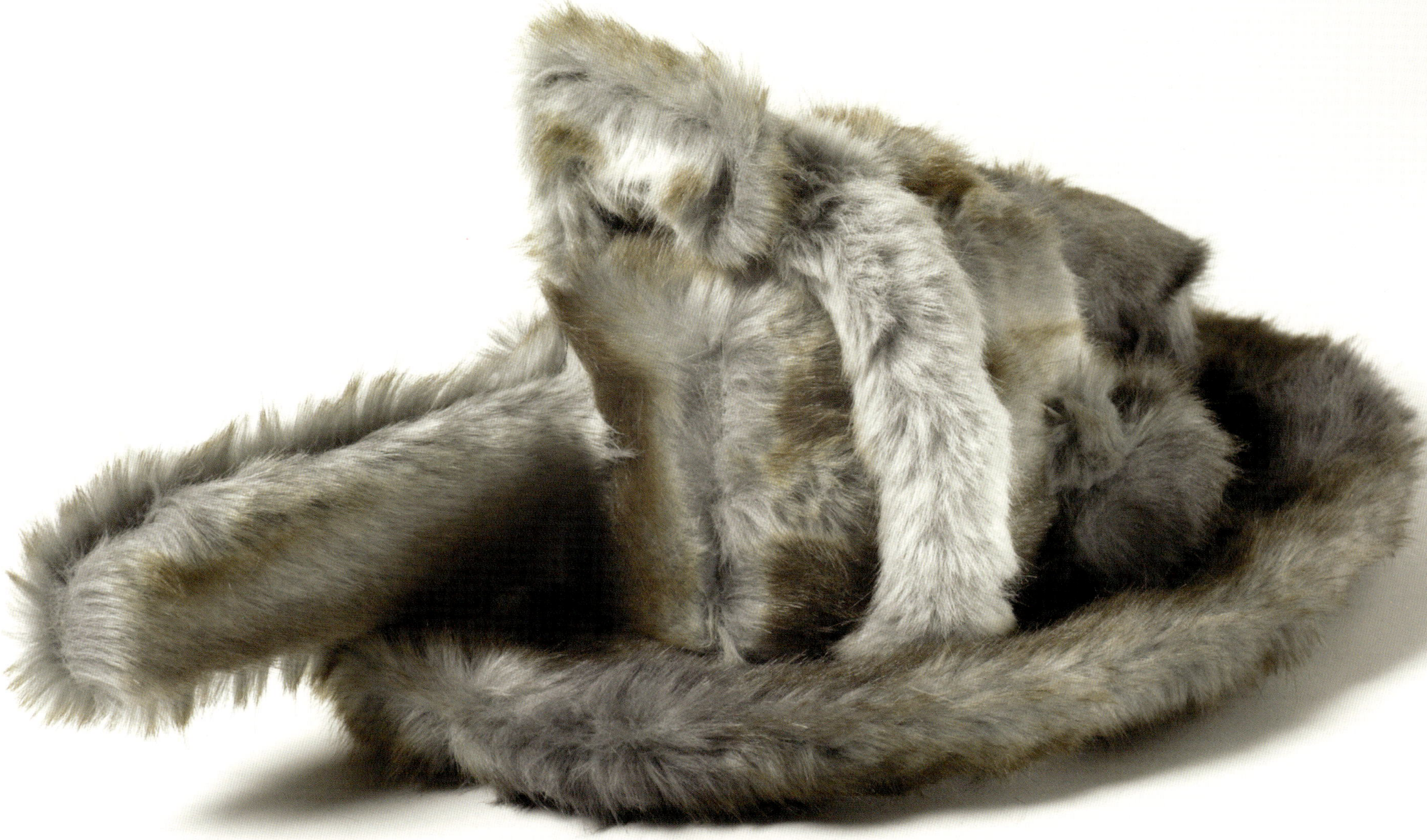

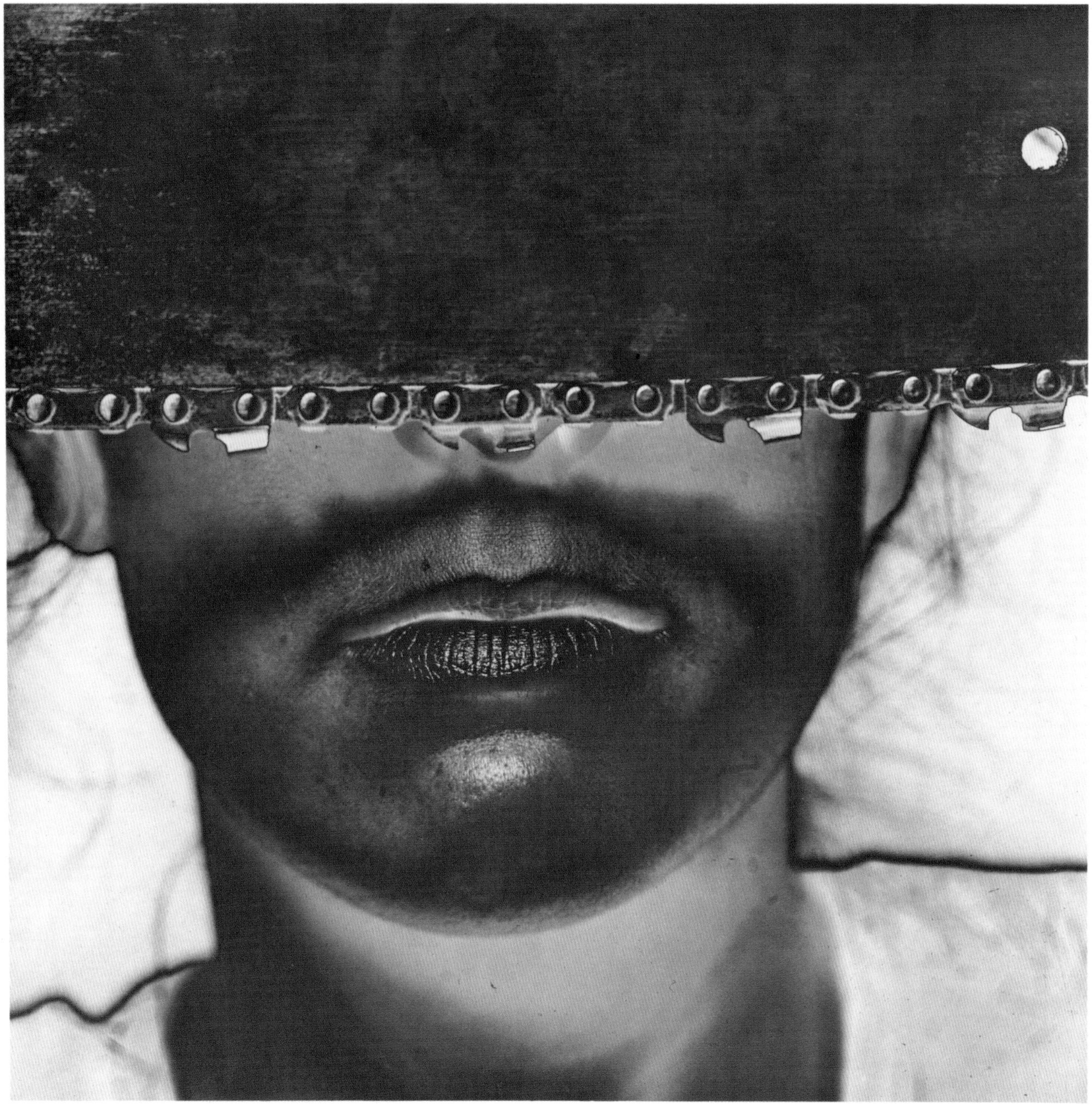

MAN RAY (1890-1976) American — ***Gaby de Montberkely***, 1951 — Gelatin silver print — 16"x 20"

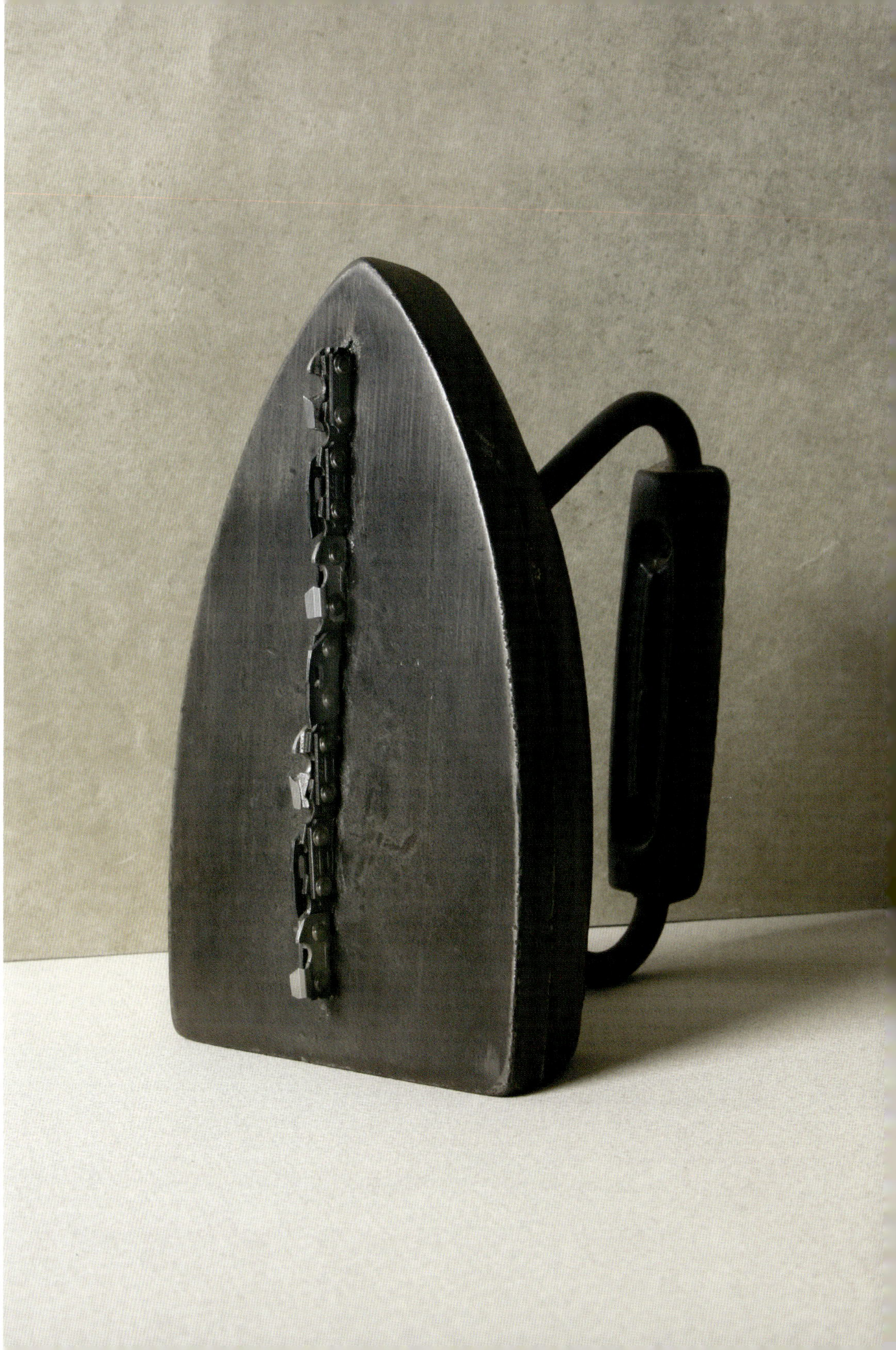

MAN RAY (1890-1976) American — ***Re-Cadeau***, 1972 — Iron and chainsaw chain — 5"x 8"

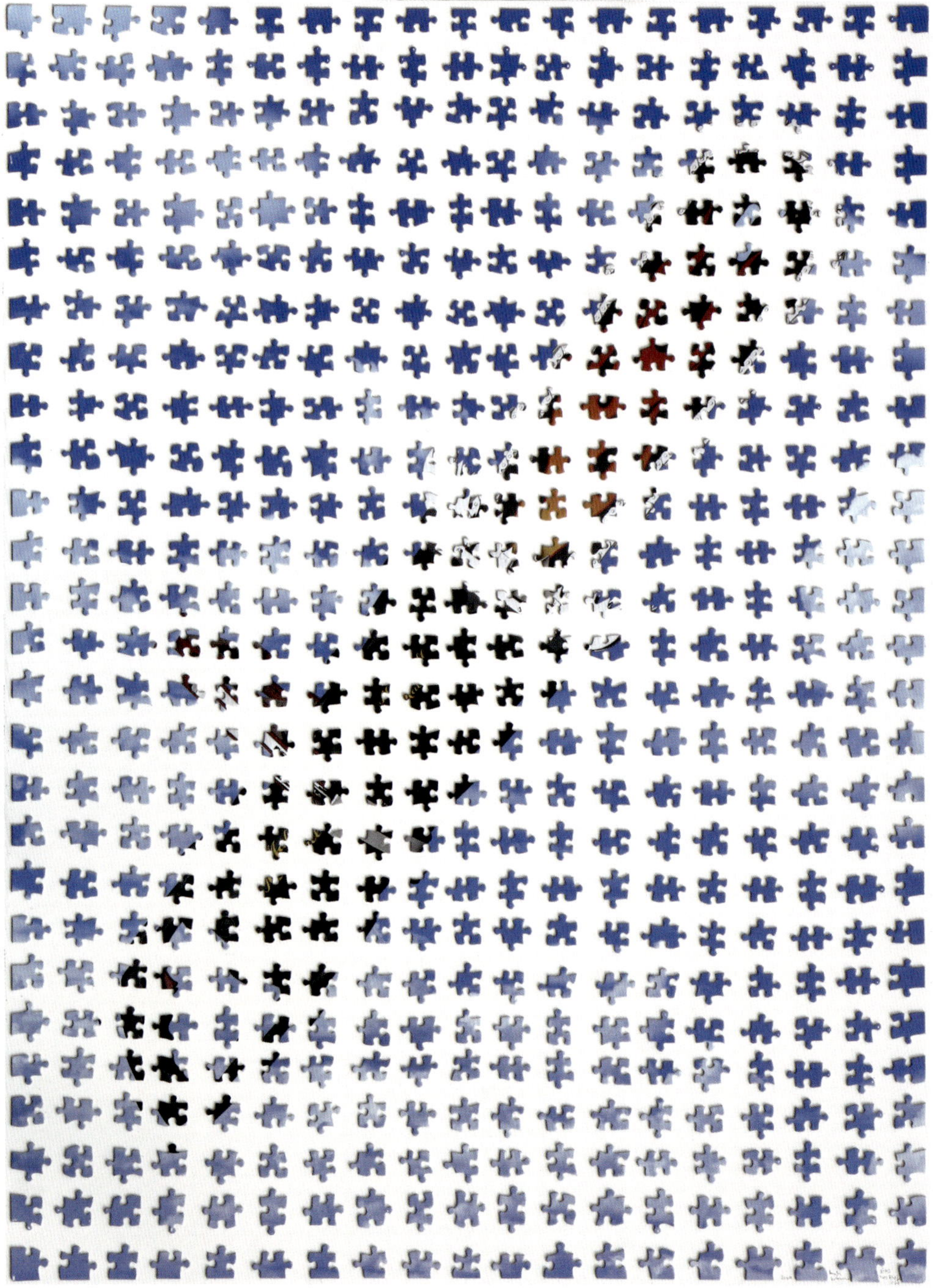

Tom Friedman (b. 1965) American — ***Untitled***, 1990 — Custom jigsaw puzzle — 30"x 40"

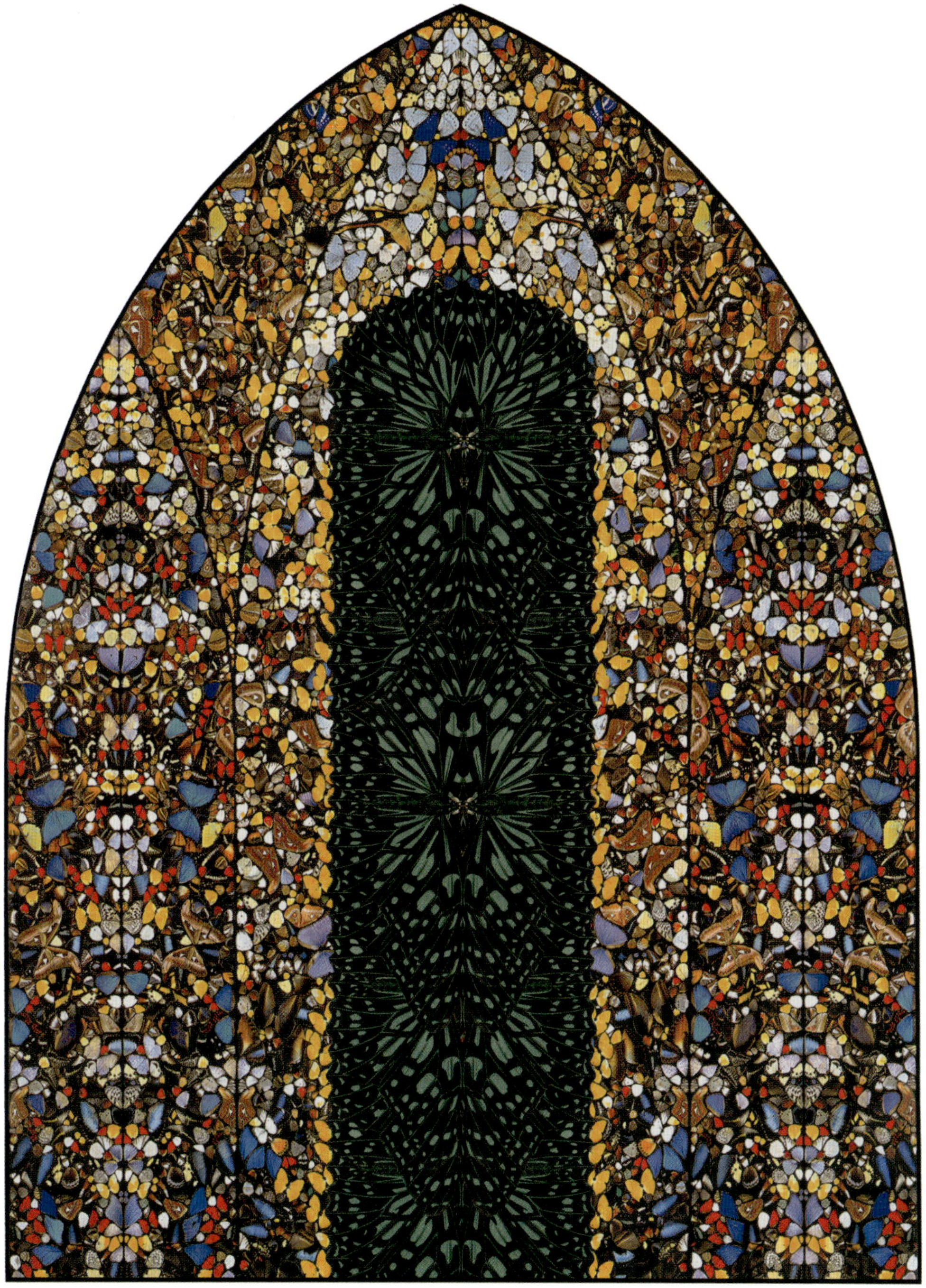

DAMIEN HIRST (b. 1965) English — ***Chainsaw in the Cathedral***, 2006 (maquette) — Digital type RA-4 print — 11"x 14"

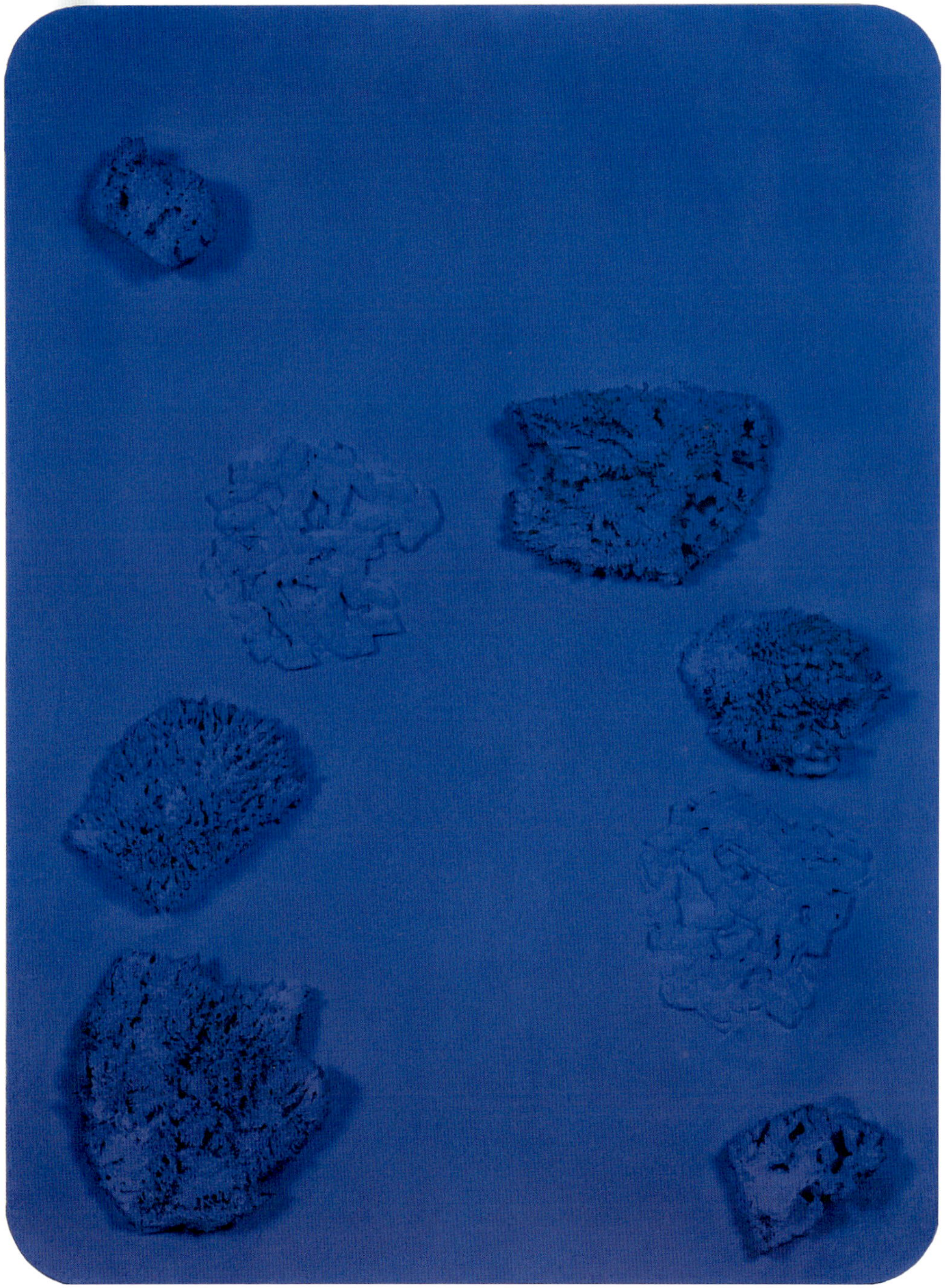

YVES KLEIN (1928-1962) French — ***Blue Monochrome Sponge Chain Relief***, 1960 — Sponges, chainsaw chain, dry pigment in synthetic resin on plywood — 18"x 24"

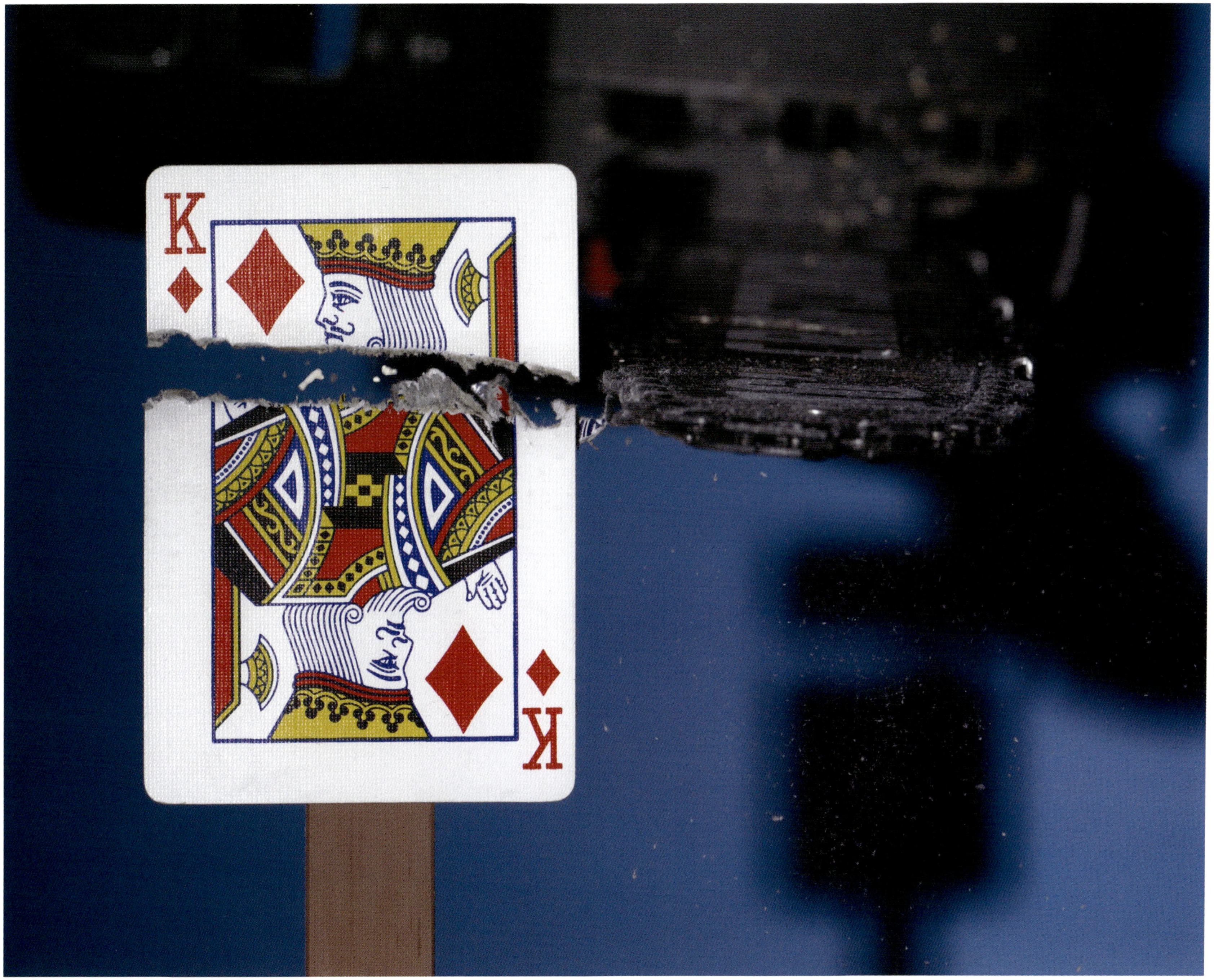

HAROLD EDGERTON (1903-1990) American — ***Cutting the Card, (not as), Quickly***, 1964 — Digital type RA-4 print — 16"x 20"

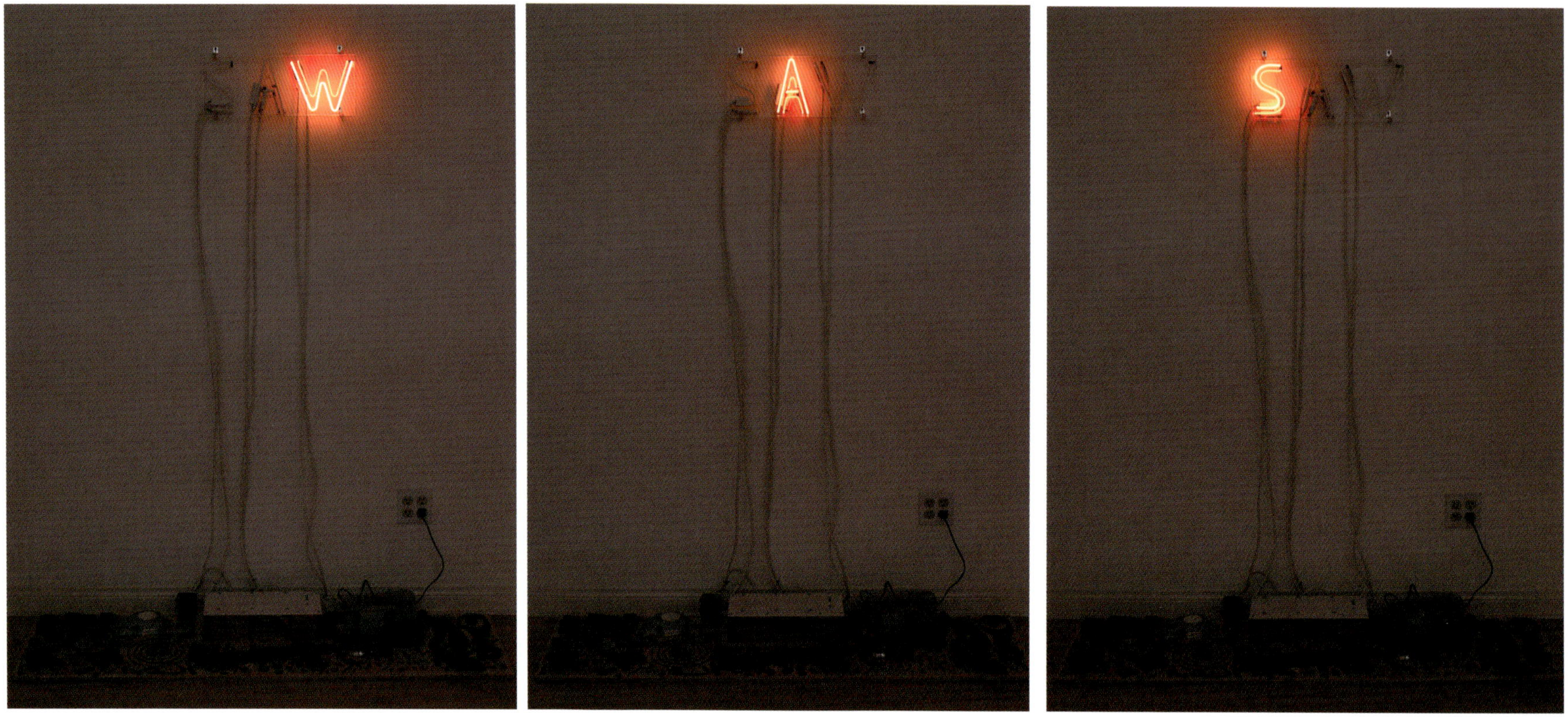

Above and facing page. BRUCE NAUMAN (b. 1941) American — ***Was/Saw,*** 1970 — Neon, glass tubing, wood, chainsaw parts, transformer, wire — 7 ¼"x 18"x 60"

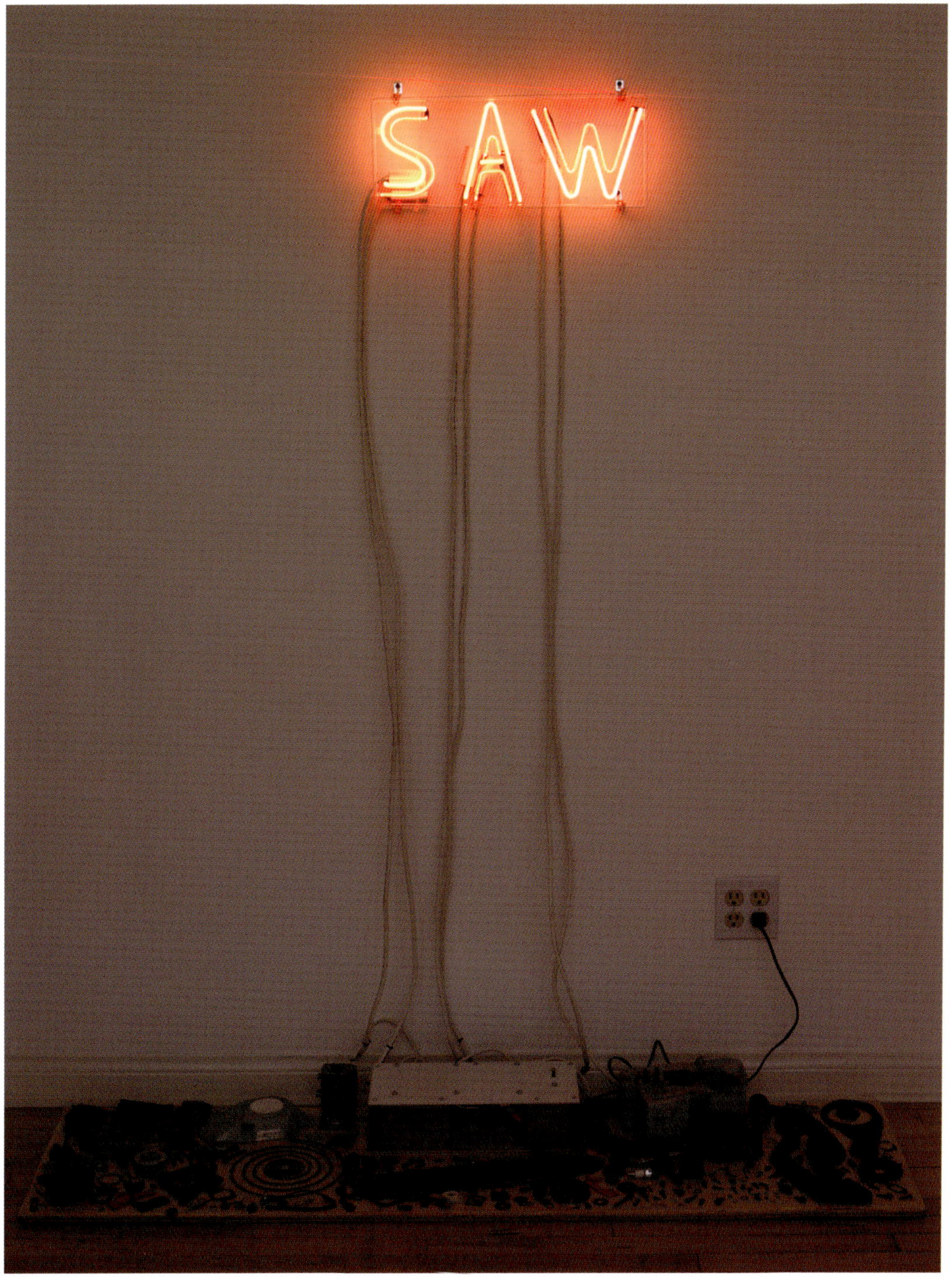
SAW

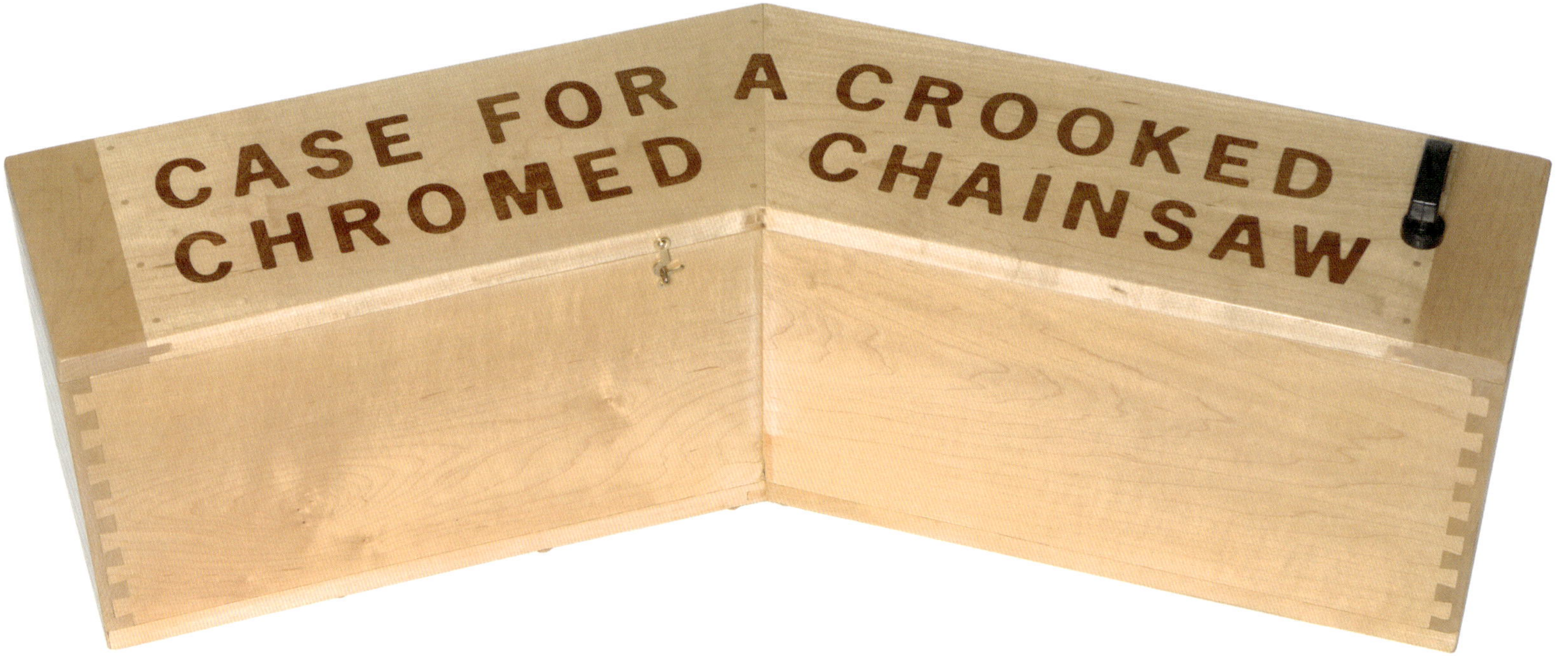
CASE FOR A CROOKED
CHROMED CHAINSAW

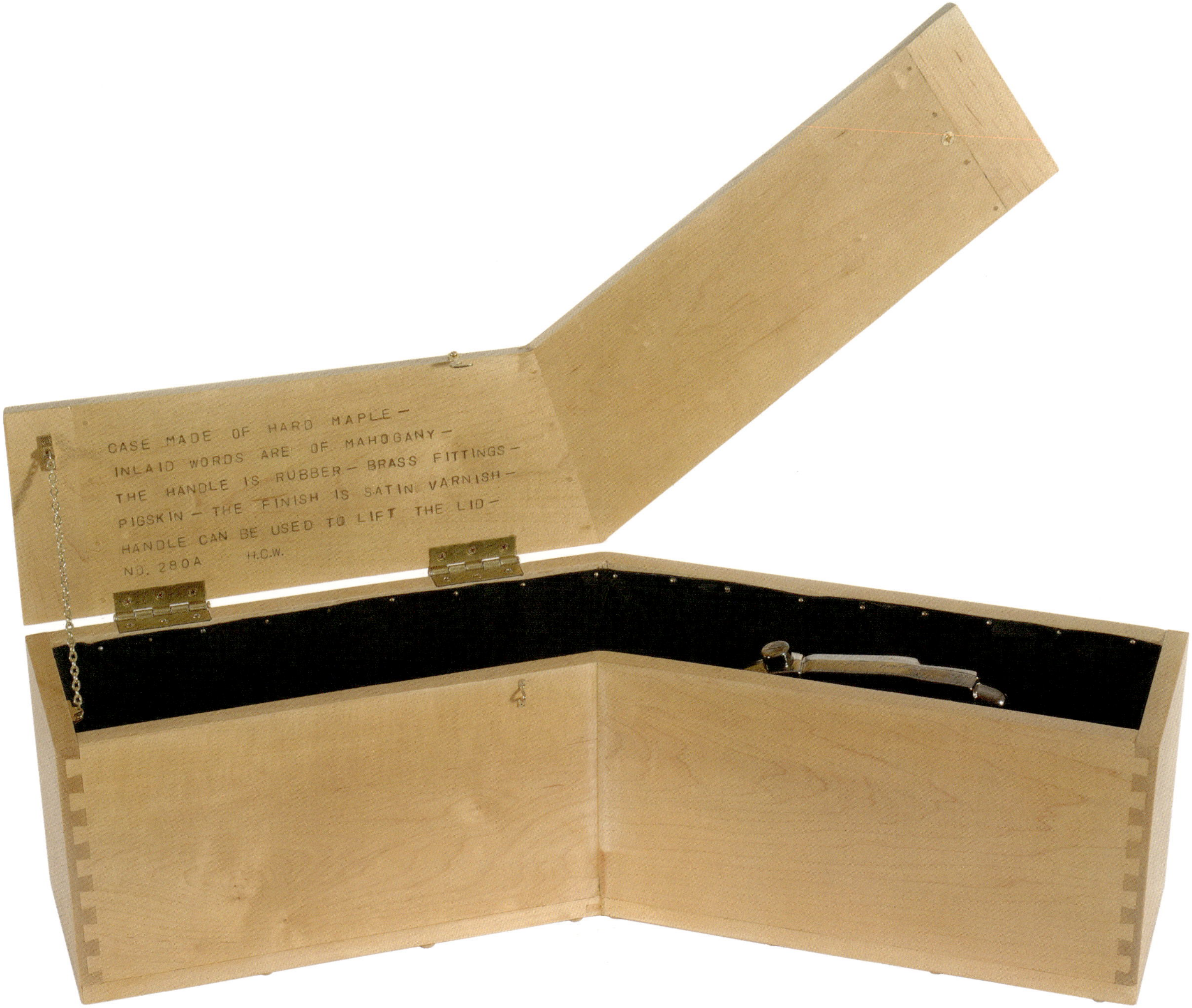

H.C. WESTERMANN (1922 - 1981) American — ***Case For A Crooked Chromed Chainsaw,*** 1979 — Hard maple, mahogany, pigskin, brass, rubber, chromed plastic chainsaw — 6”x 8 ½”x 32”

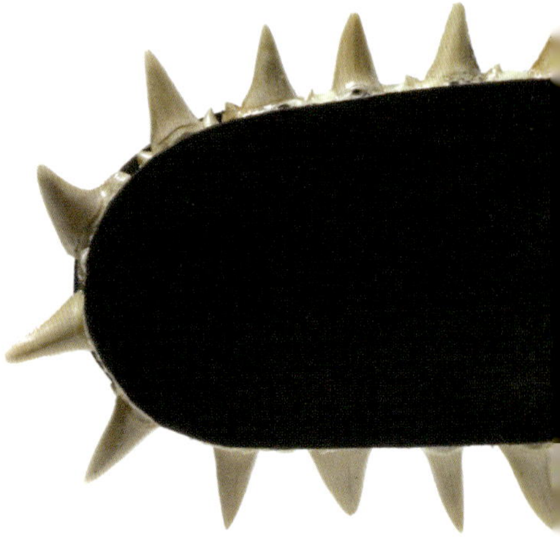

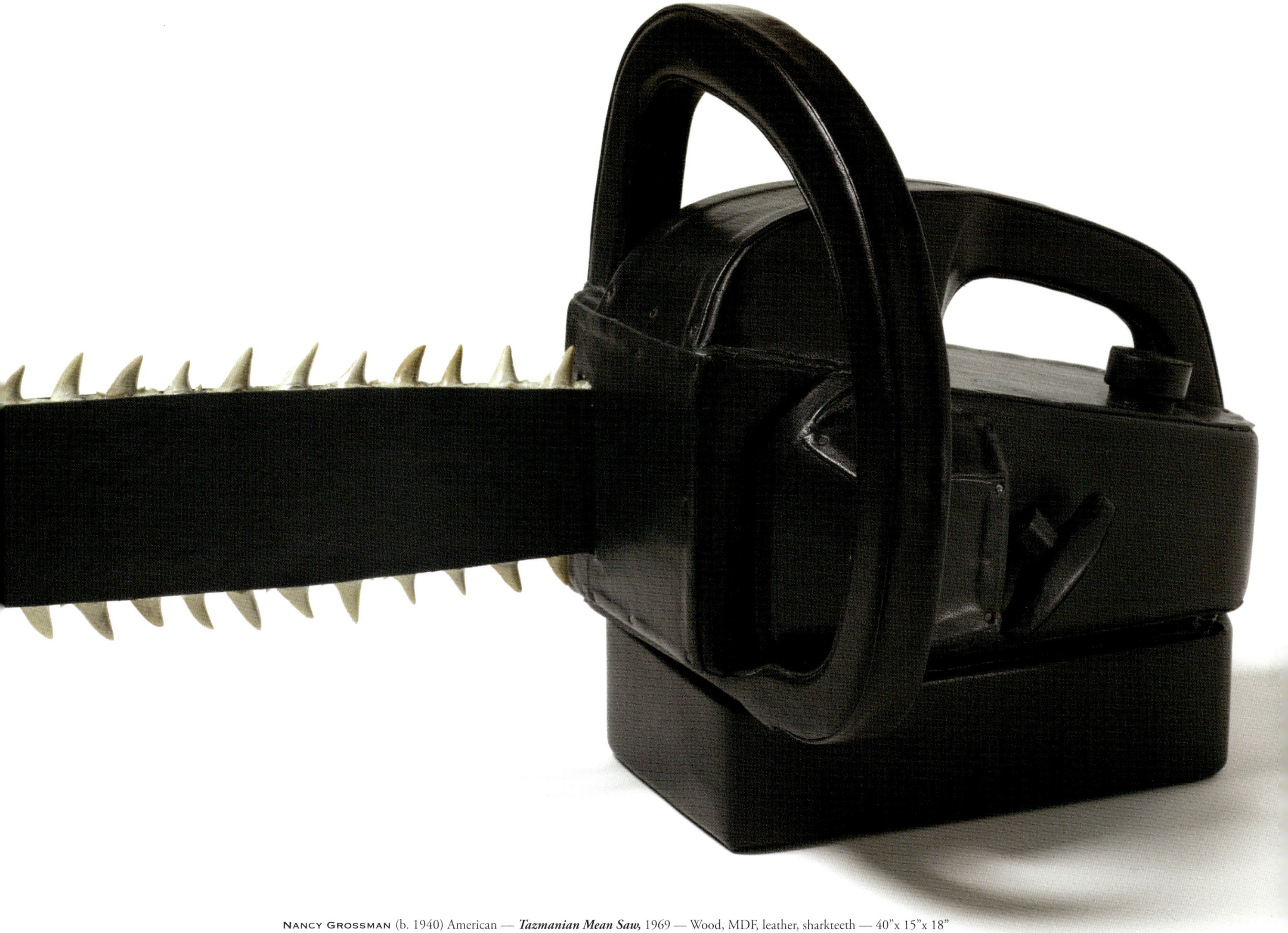

Nancy Grossman (b. 1940) American — ***Tazmanian Mean Saw,*** 1969 — Wood, MDF, leather, sharkteeth — 40"x 15"x 18"

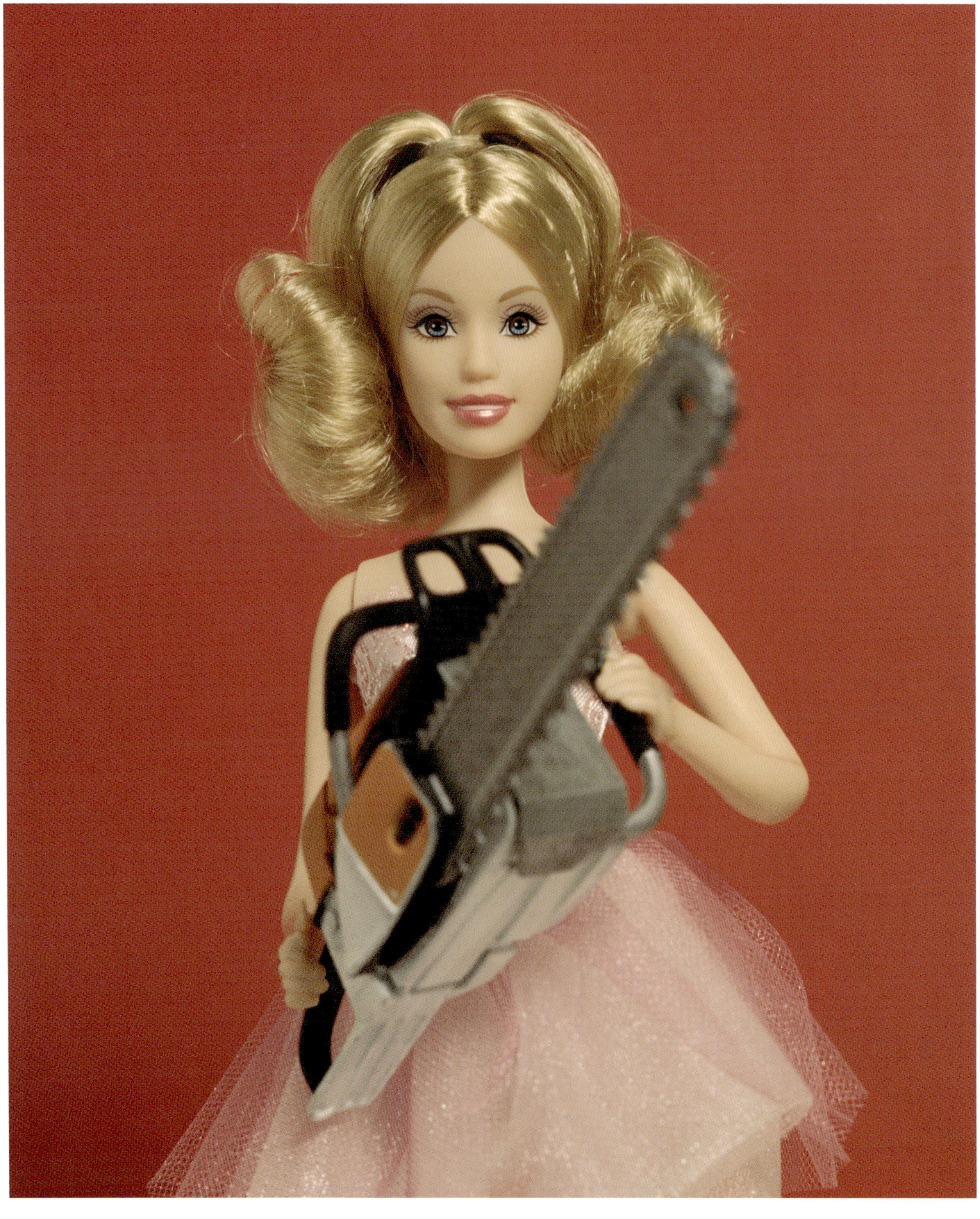

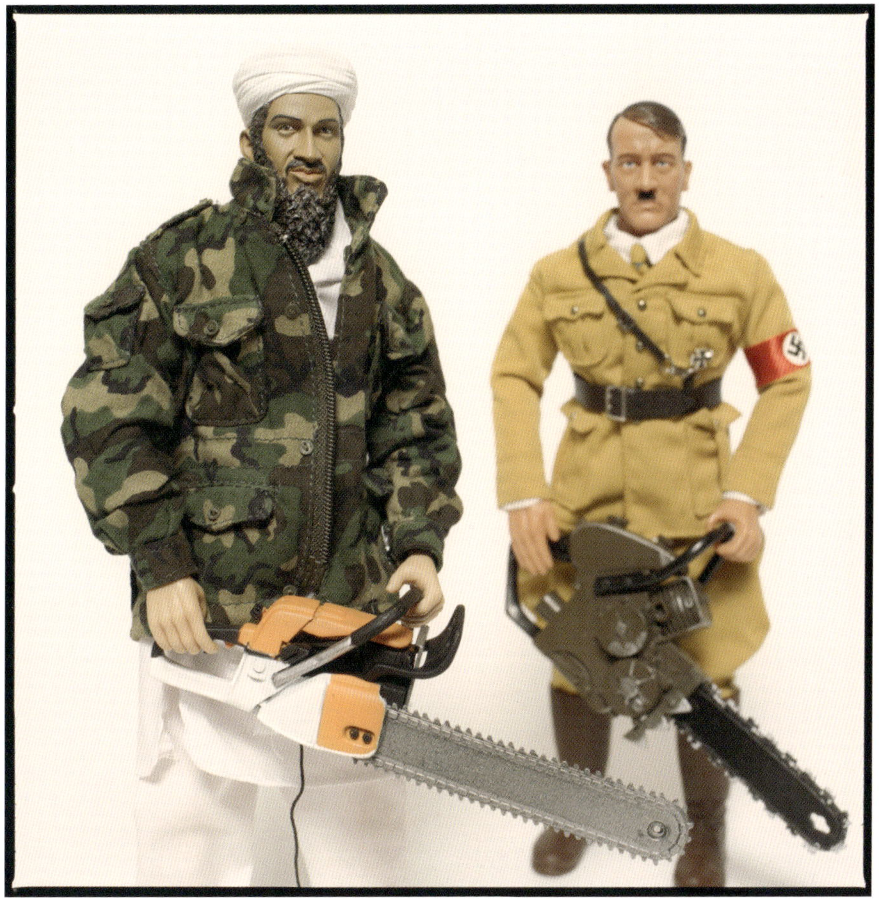

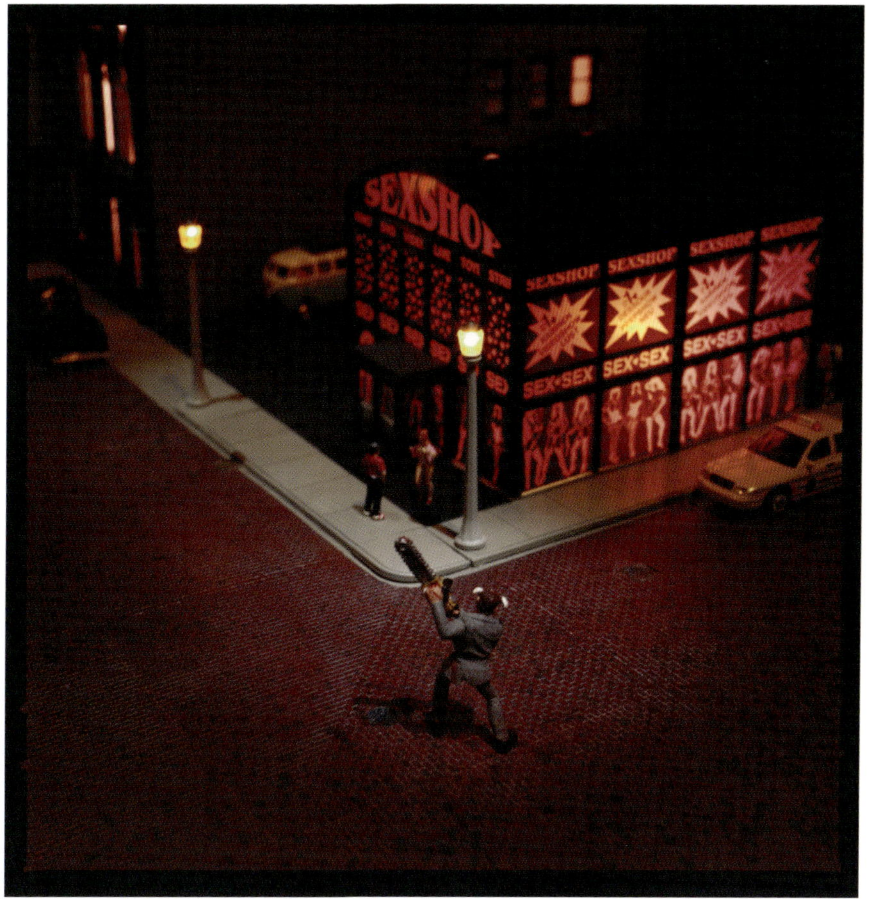

Facing page. DAVID LEVINTHAL (b. 1949) American — ***Barbie saw,*** 1997 — Digital type RA-4 print — 20"x 24"

Left. DAVID LEVINTHAL (b. 1949) American — ***Who Would Win? from "Mein Quampf,"*** 1993 — Digital type RA-4 print — 20"x 24"

Right. DAVID LEVINTHAL (b. 1949) American — ***Uh-Oh, from "Modern Romance,"*** 1997 — Digital type RA-4 print — 20"x 24"

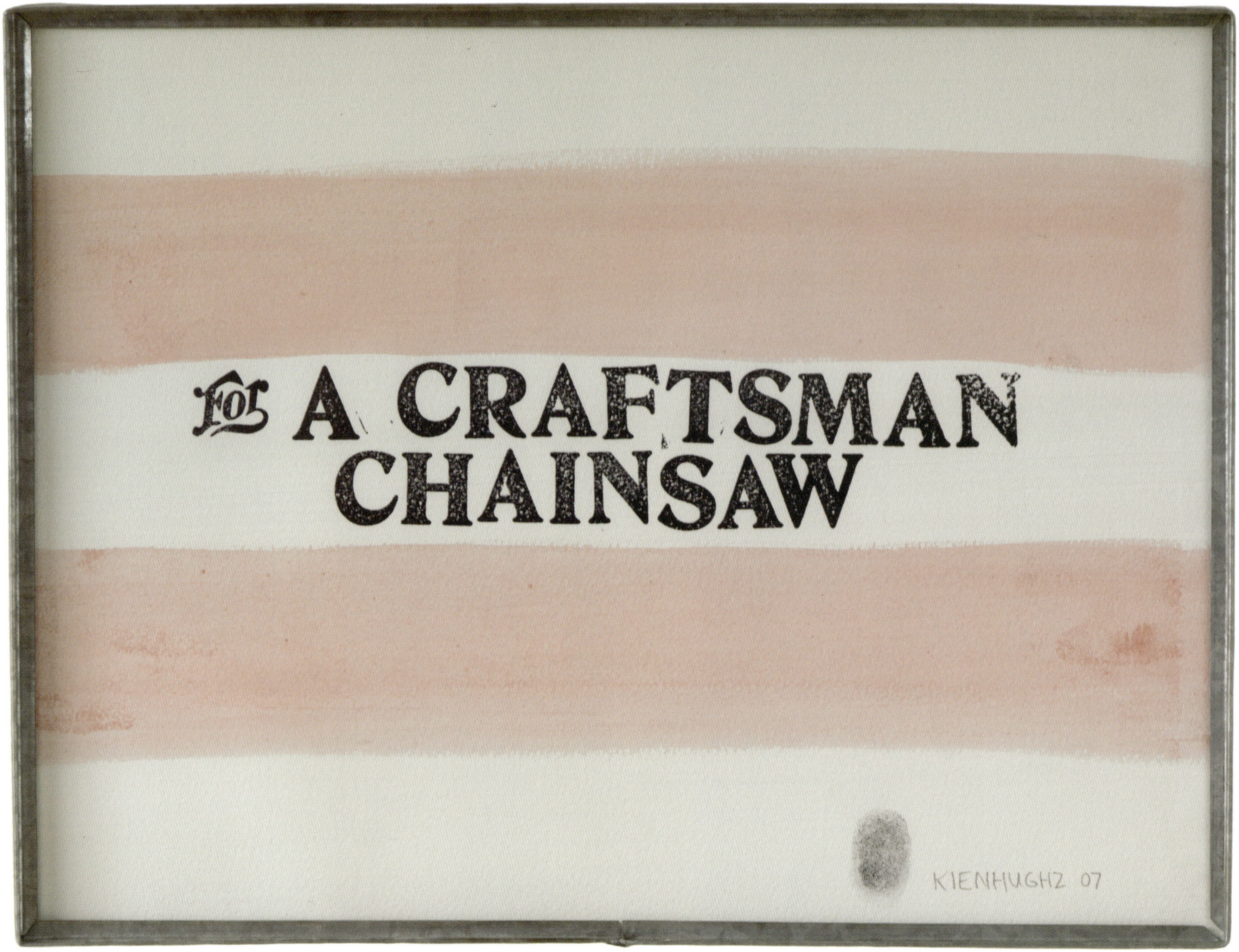

Ed Kienholz (1927 - 1994) American — ***For Craftsman Chainsaw***, 2007 — Watercolor, rubber stamp ink on paper, galvanized steel, particle board — 12"x 16"

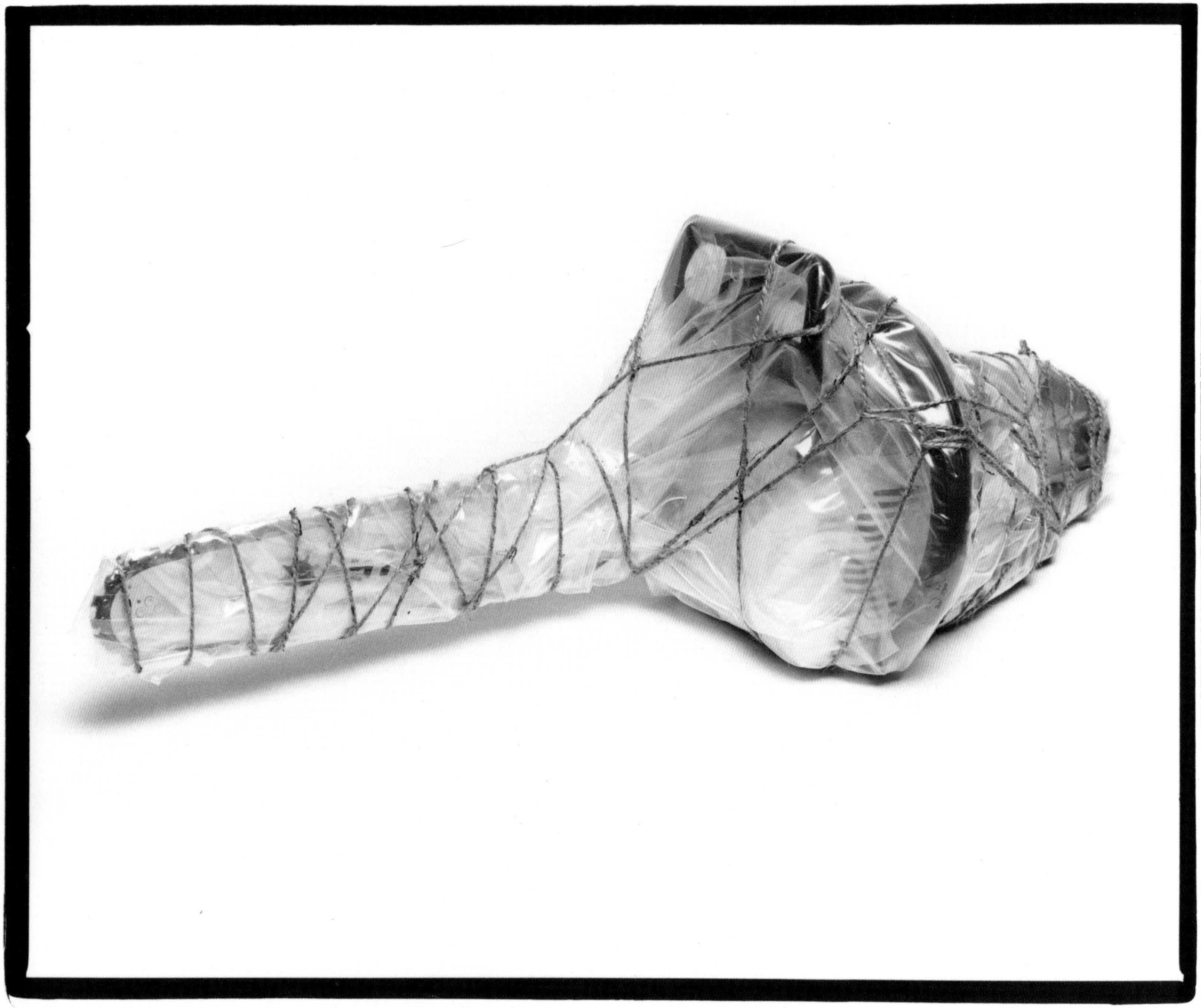

CHRISTO (b. 1935) Bulgarian — ***Wrapped Chainsaw,*** 1990 (Original lost) — Gelatin silver print — 16"x 20"

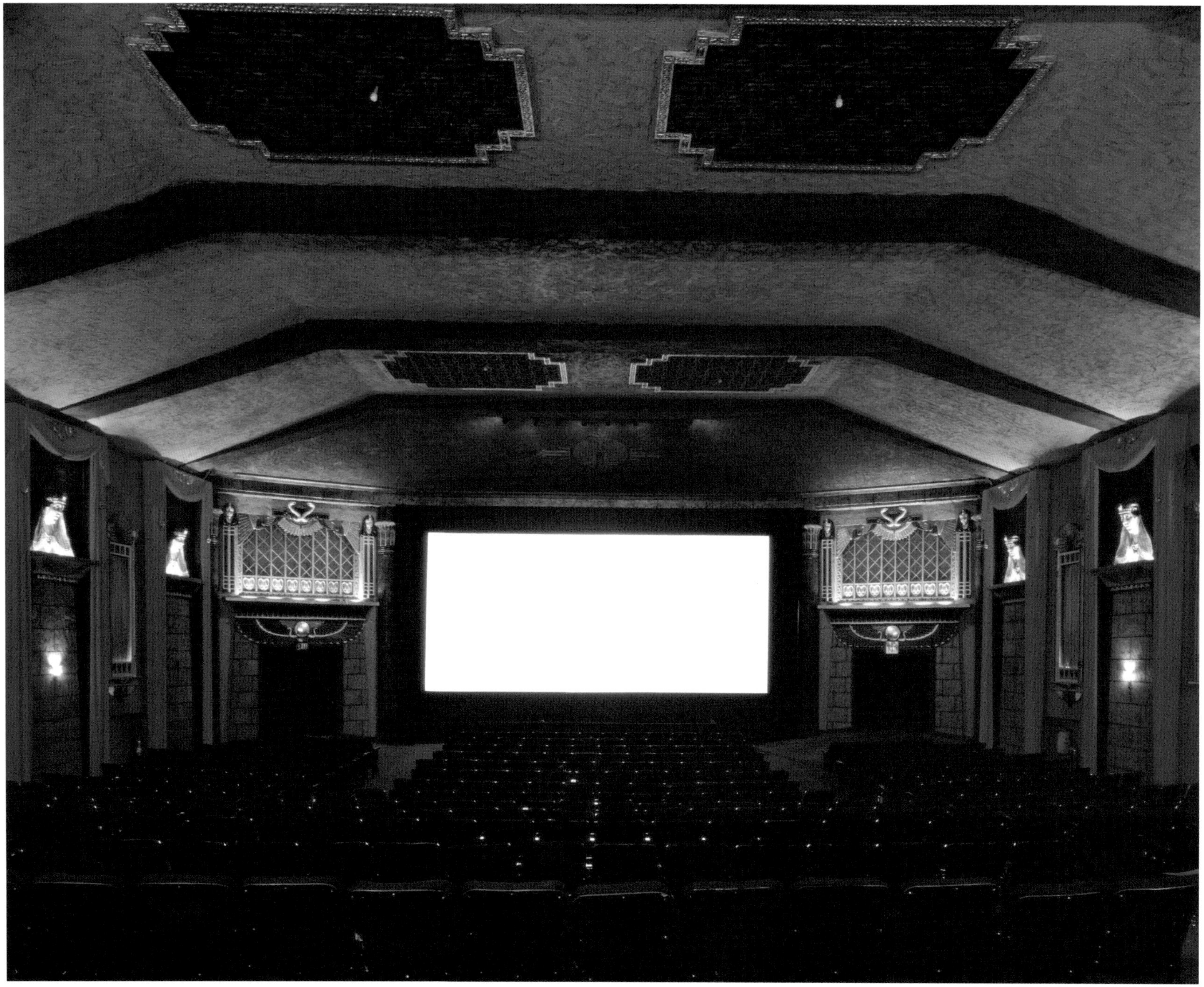

HIROSHI SUGIMOTO (b. 1948) Japanese — ***Vista Theatre (Texas Chainsaw Massacre 2)***, 1992 — Gelatin silver print — 16"x 20"

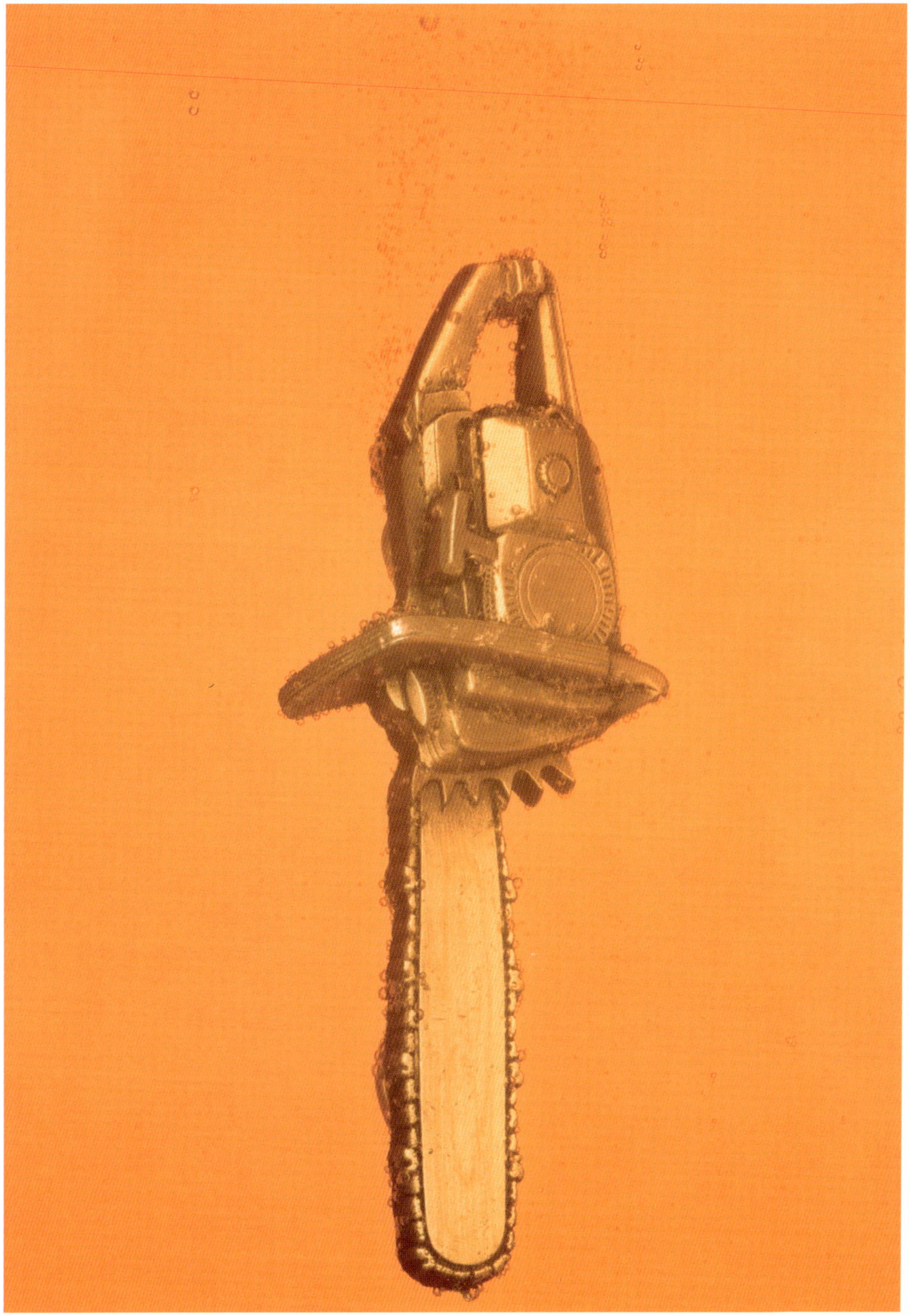

ANDRES SERRANO (b. 1950) American — ***Piss Saw,*** 1987 — Archival inkjet print on paper — 24"x 30"

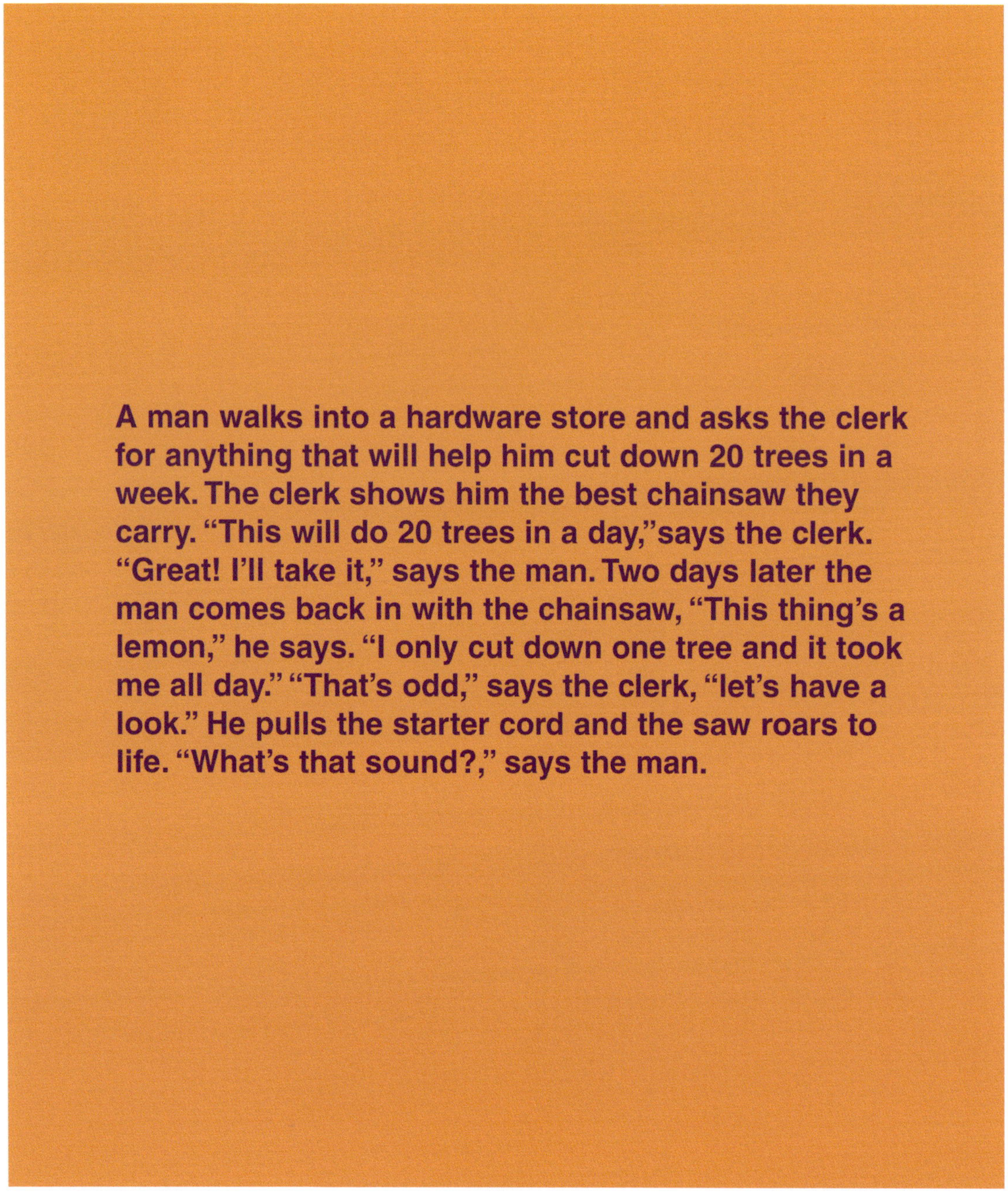

RICHARD PRINCE (b. 1949) American — ***Untitled (Man walks into a hardware store),*** 1987 — Acrylic and silkscreen ink on canvas — 48"x 60"

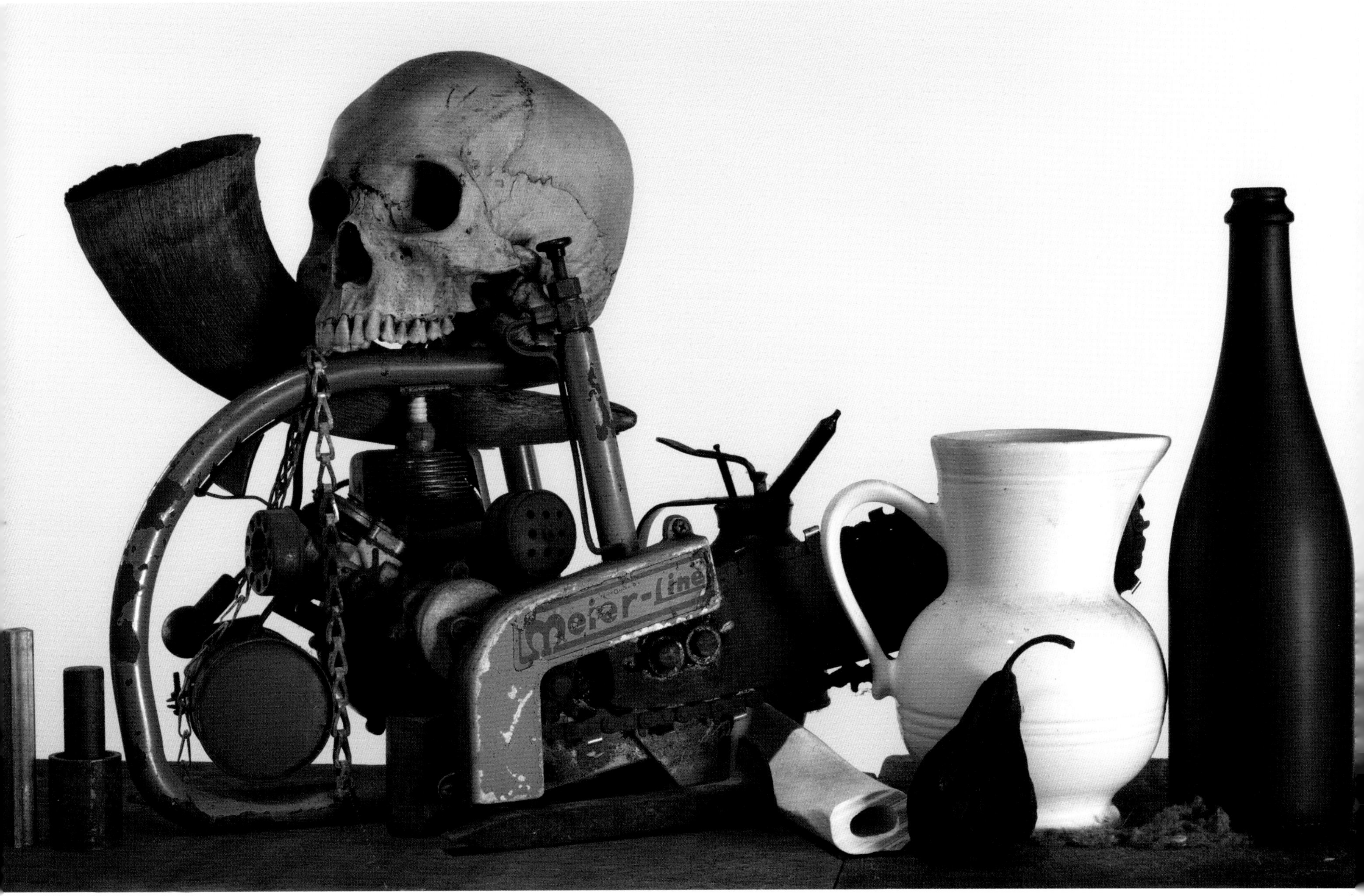

IRVING PENN (b. 1917) American — ***Composition with Skull and Pear,*** 1979 — Platinum/palladium print on paper — 16"x 20"

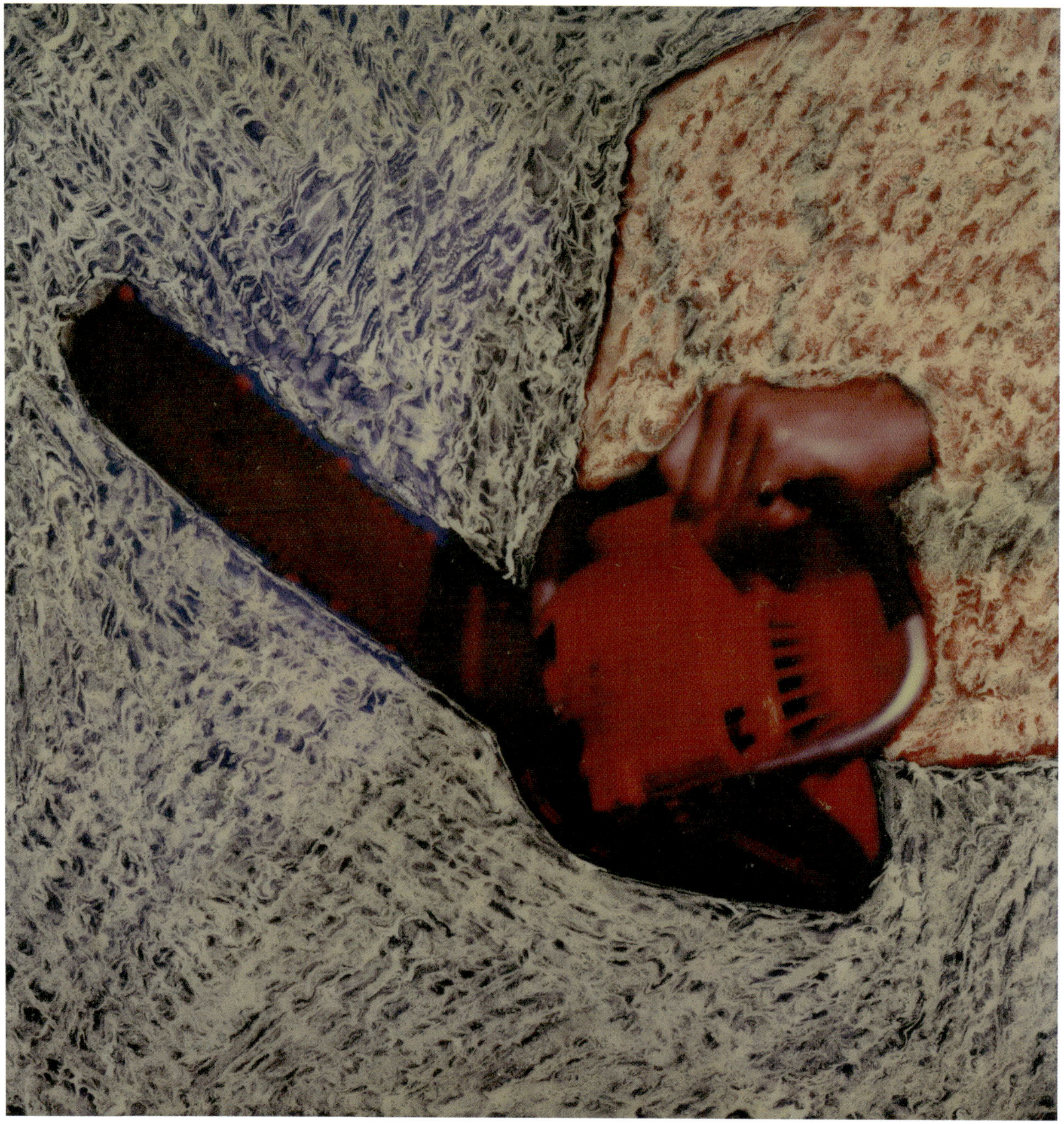

LUCAS SAMARAS (b. 1936) American — ***Photo-Transformation,*** December 13, 1974 — Altered polaroid film — 4"x 5"

Facing page. ARNULF RAINER (b. 1929) Austrian — ***Untitled***, 1977 — Digital type RA-4 print, oil crayon — 16"x 20"

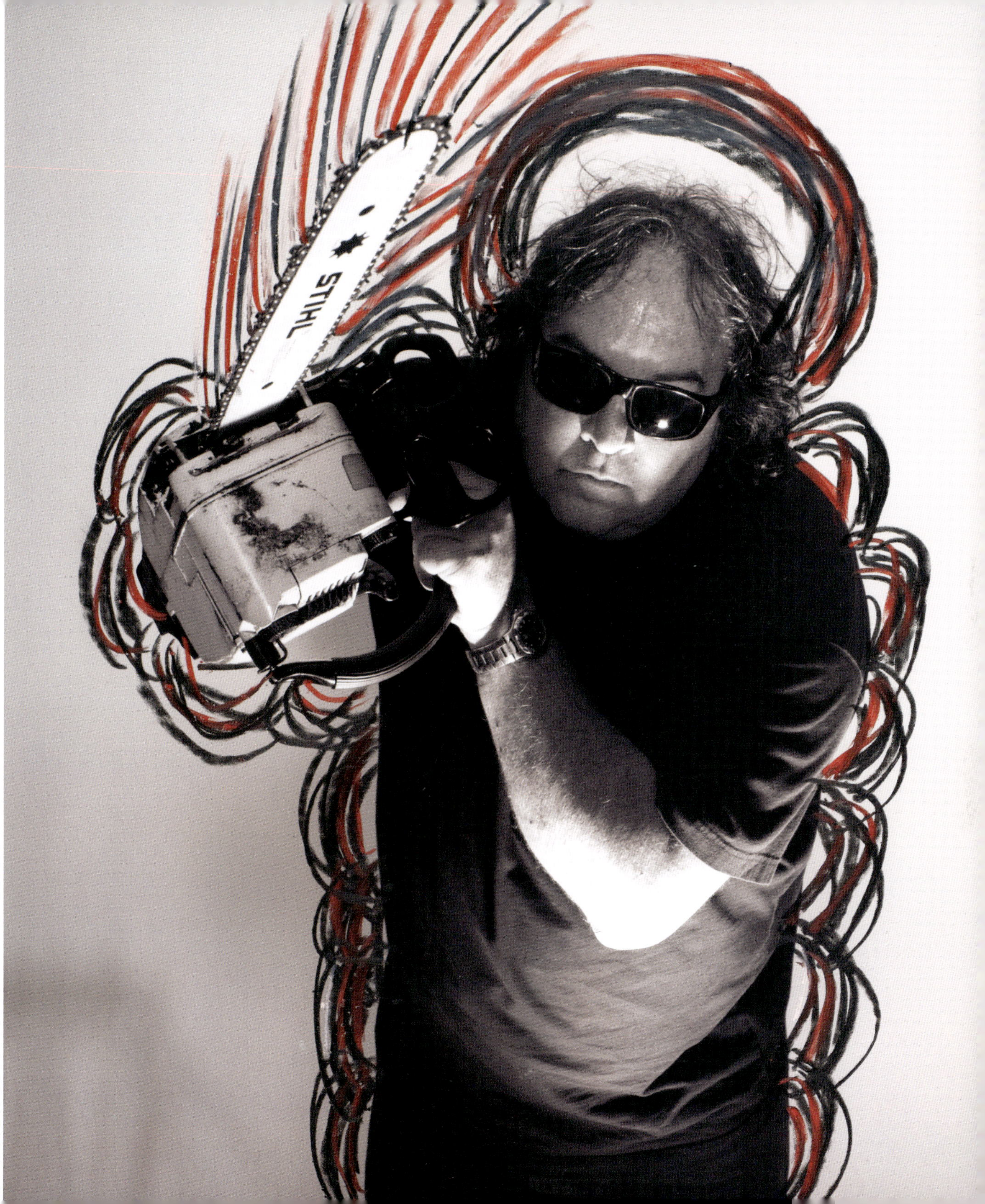
STIHL

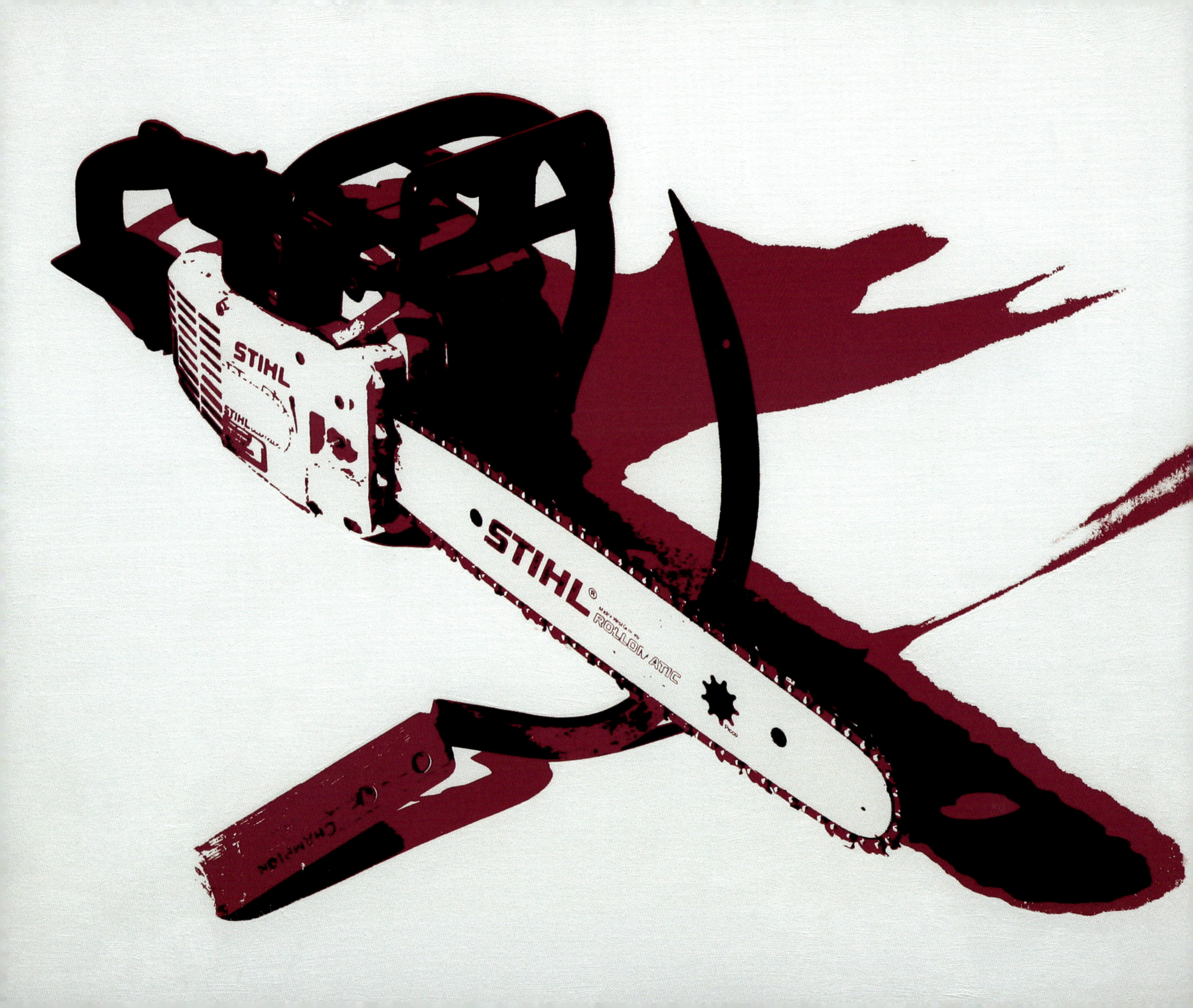
STIHL
STIHL

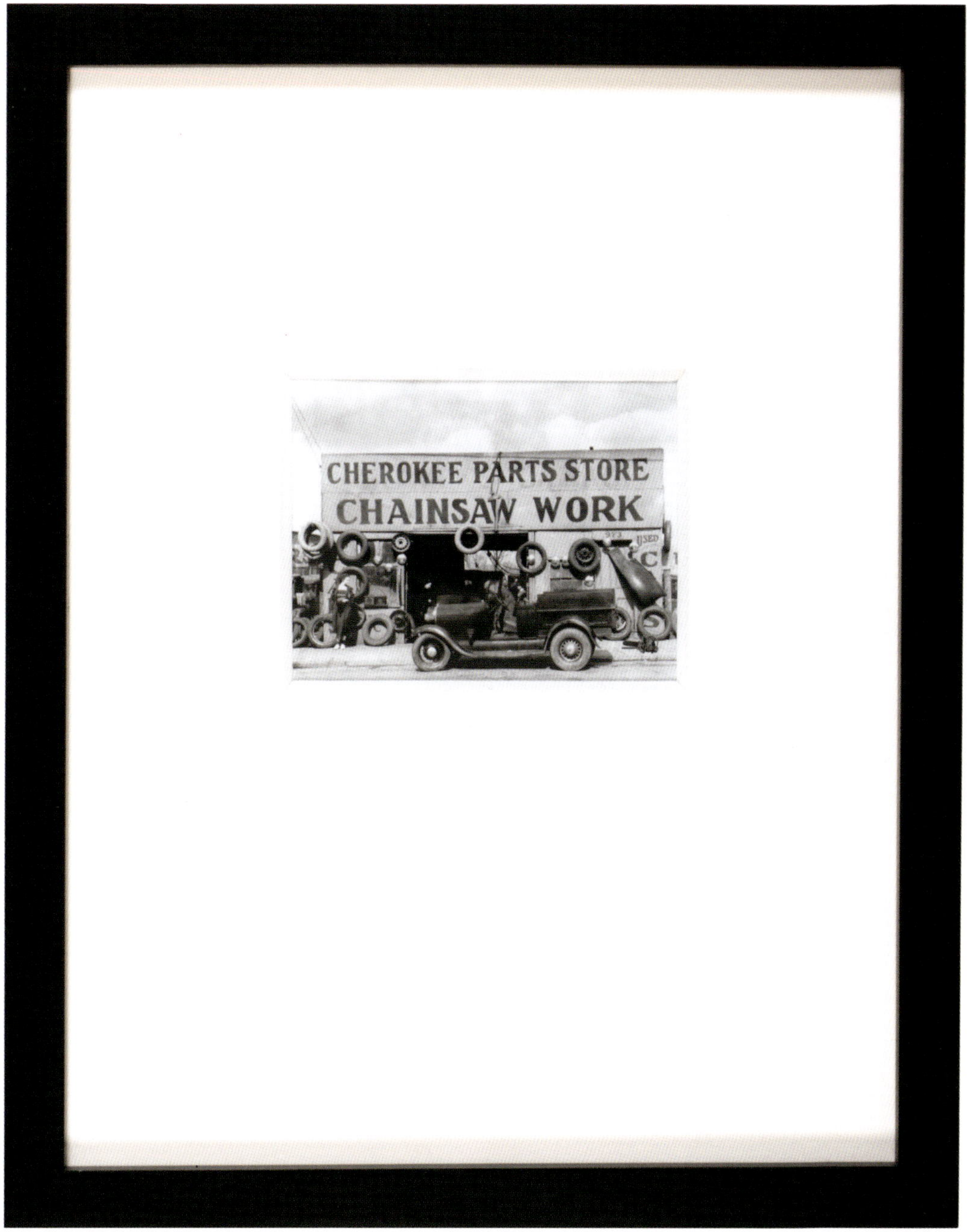

Facing page. ELAINE STURTEVANT (b. 1930) American — ***Warhol Chainsaw and Sickle,*** 1976 — Screenprint and acrylic on canvas — 24"x 30"

SHERRIE LEVINE (b. 1947) American — ***After Walker Evans #23,*** 1980 — Archival inkjet print on paper — 4"x 5"

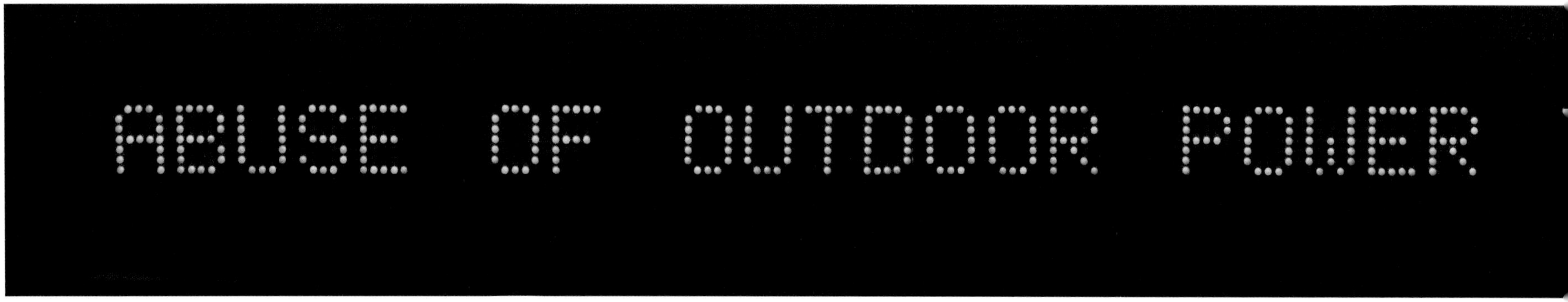

Jenny Holzer (b. 1950) American — ***Abuse of Outdoor Power Tools Comes As No Surprise,*** 1980 — LED display — 30"x 5"x 2"

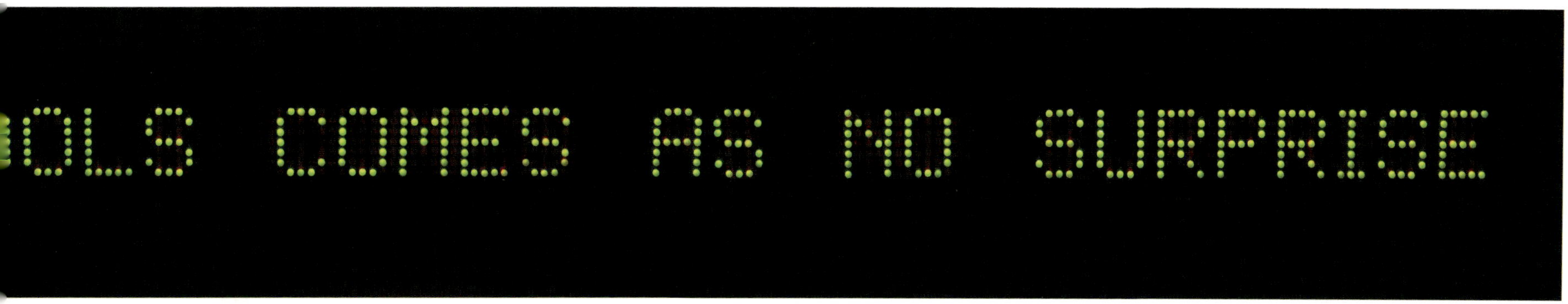
OLS COMES AS NO SURPRISE

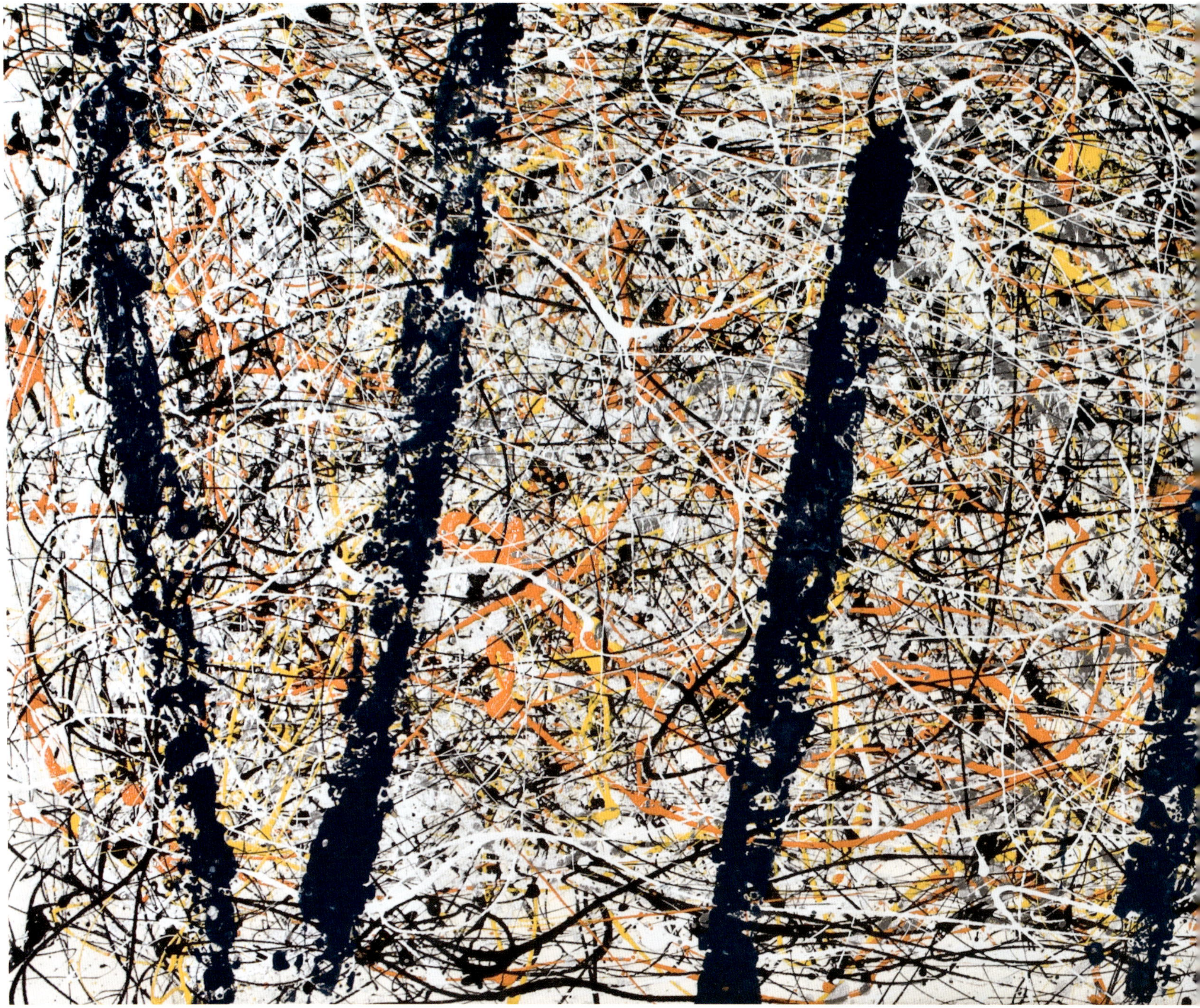

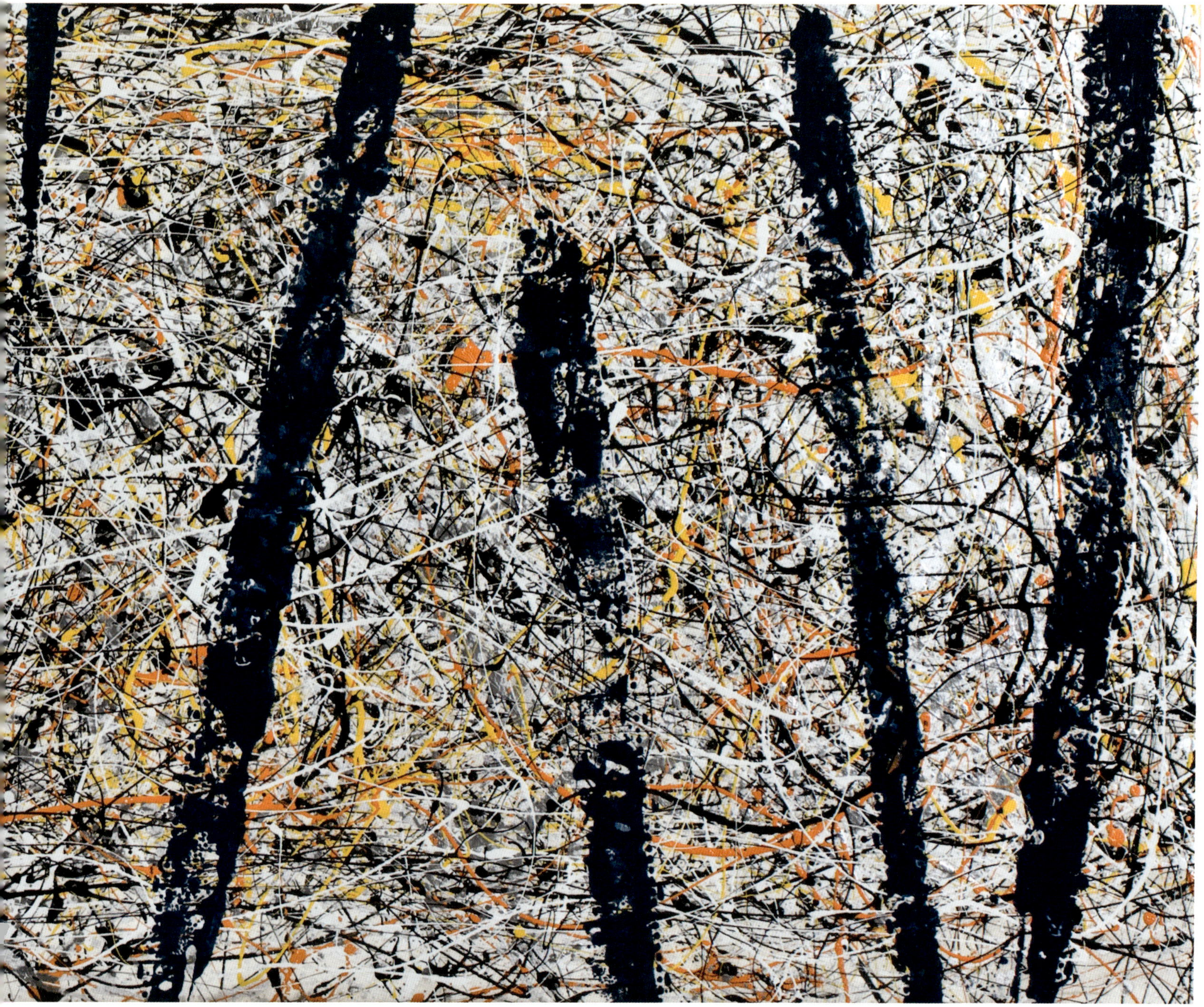

Jackson Pollock (1912 - 1956) American — ***Blue Bars***, 1952 — Enamel, aluminum paint and oil on canvas — 36"x 96"

ALLEGEDLY EXHIBITION

al • leged (ə-lĕjd, ə-lĕj′ĭd) *adj.* Represented as existing or as being as described but not so proved; supposed. — **al • leg′ed • ly** (ə-lĕj′ĭd-lē) *adv.*

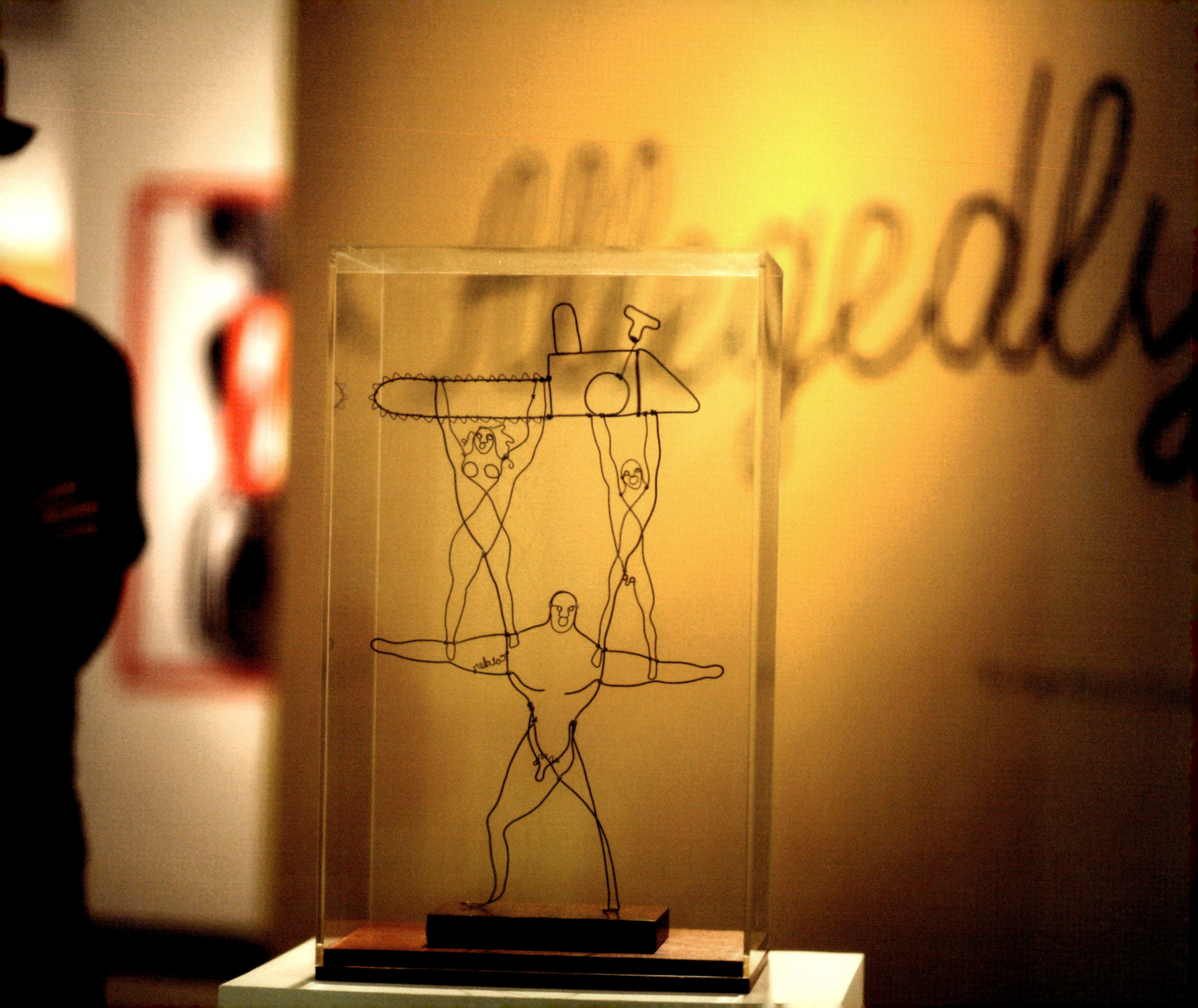

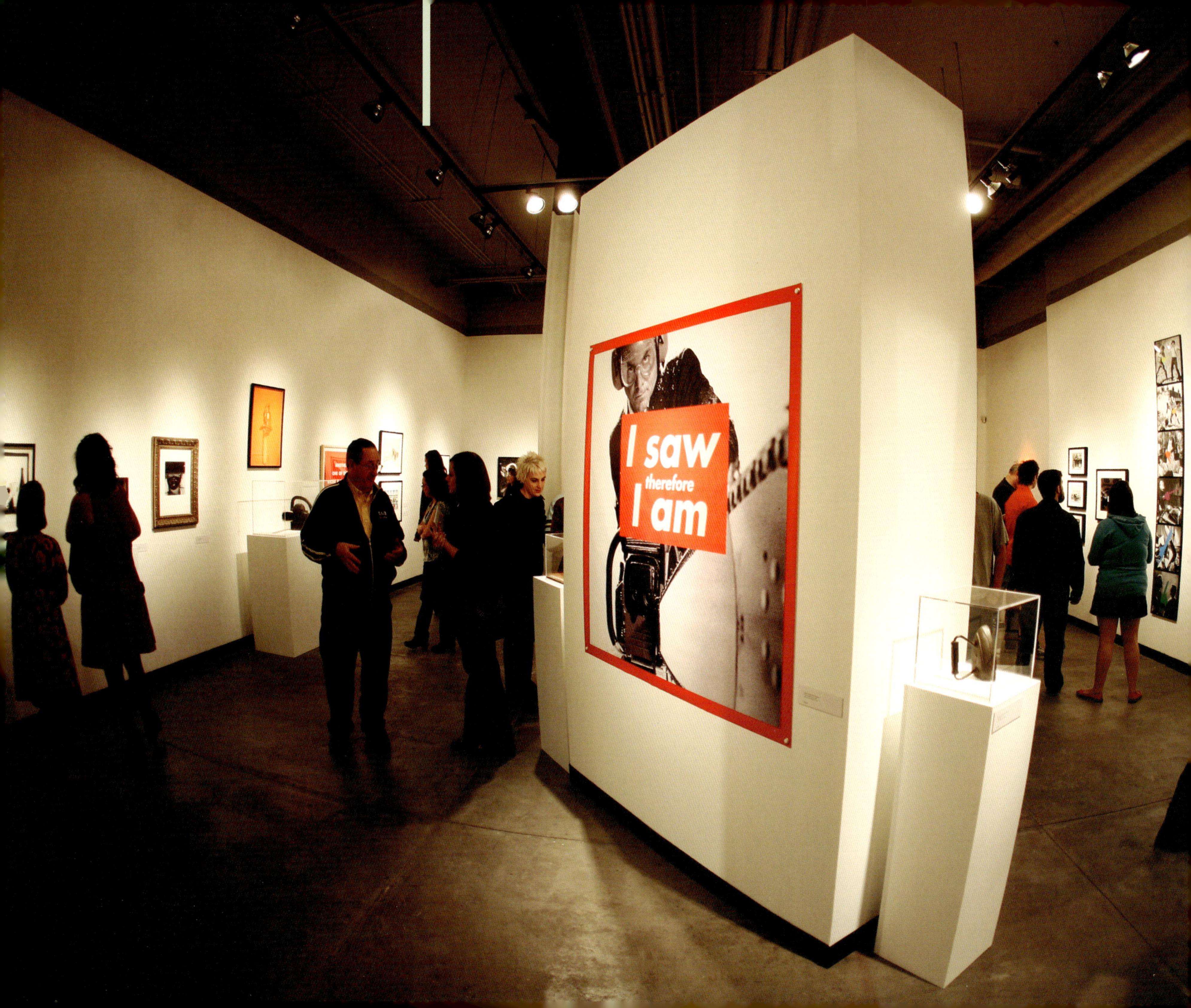
I saw
therefore
I am

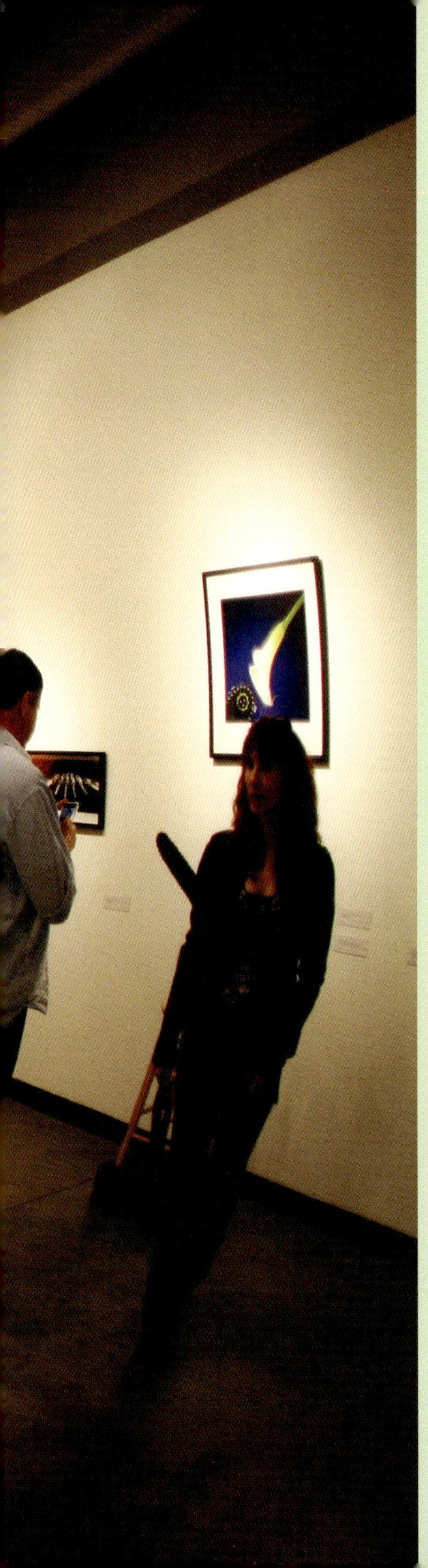

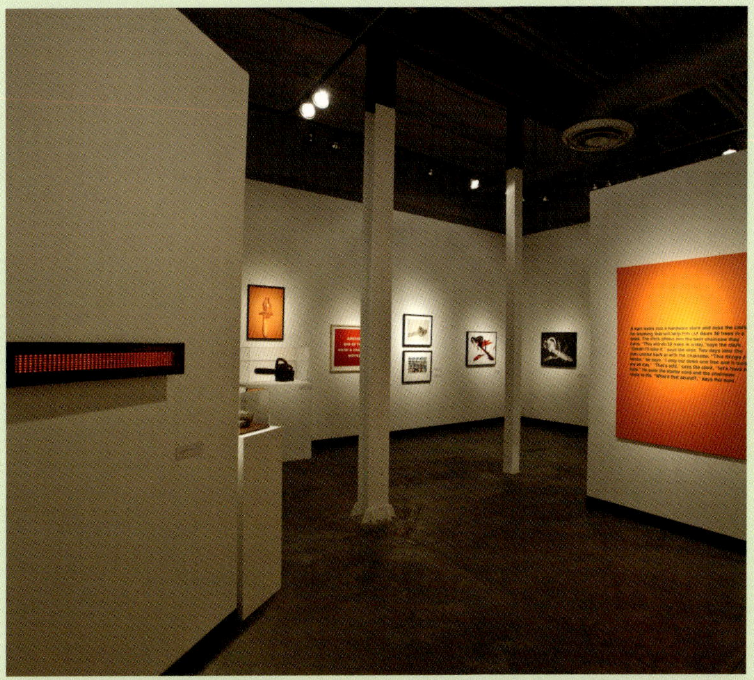

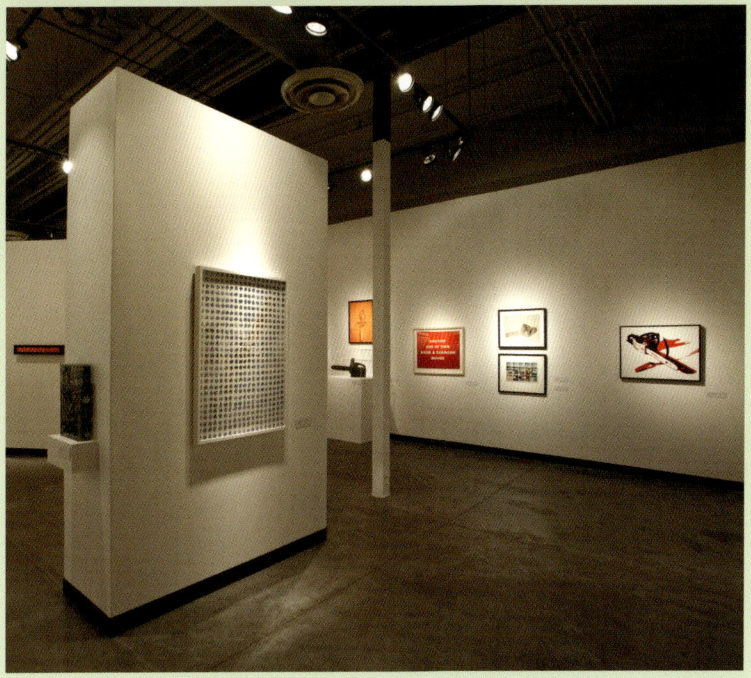

GRAND CENTRAL ART CENTER — May 2 - June 14, 2009

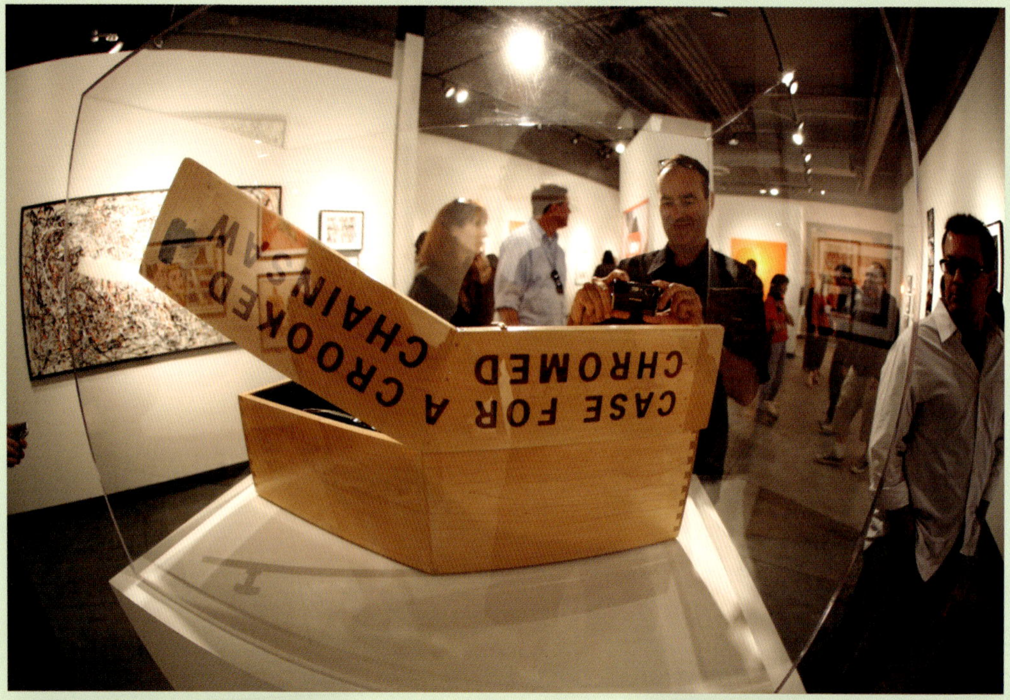
CASE FOR A CROOKED
CHROMED
CHAINSAW

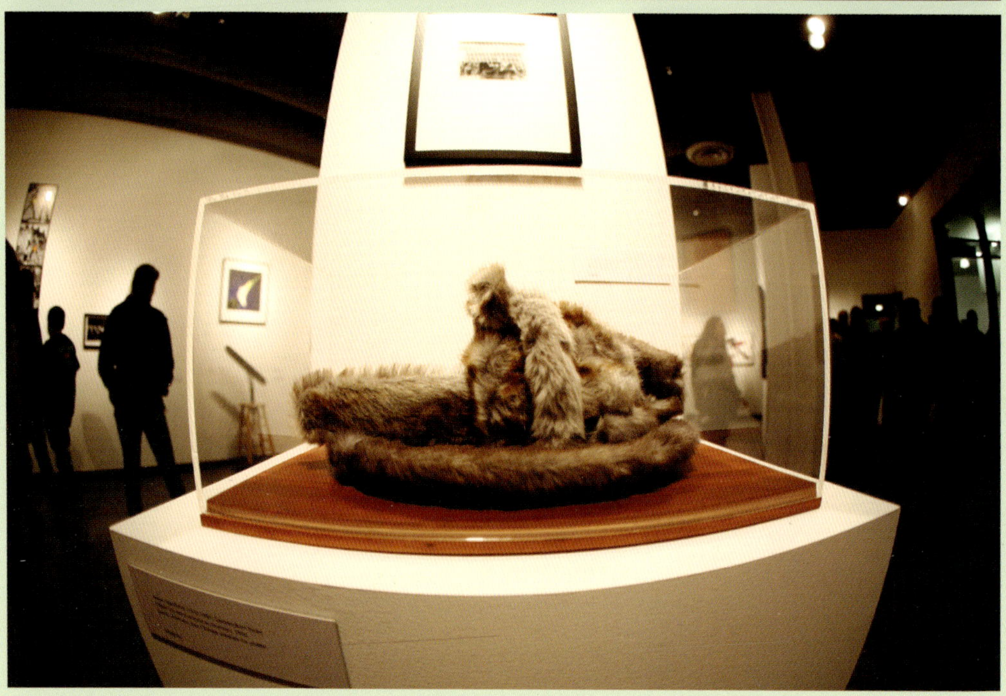

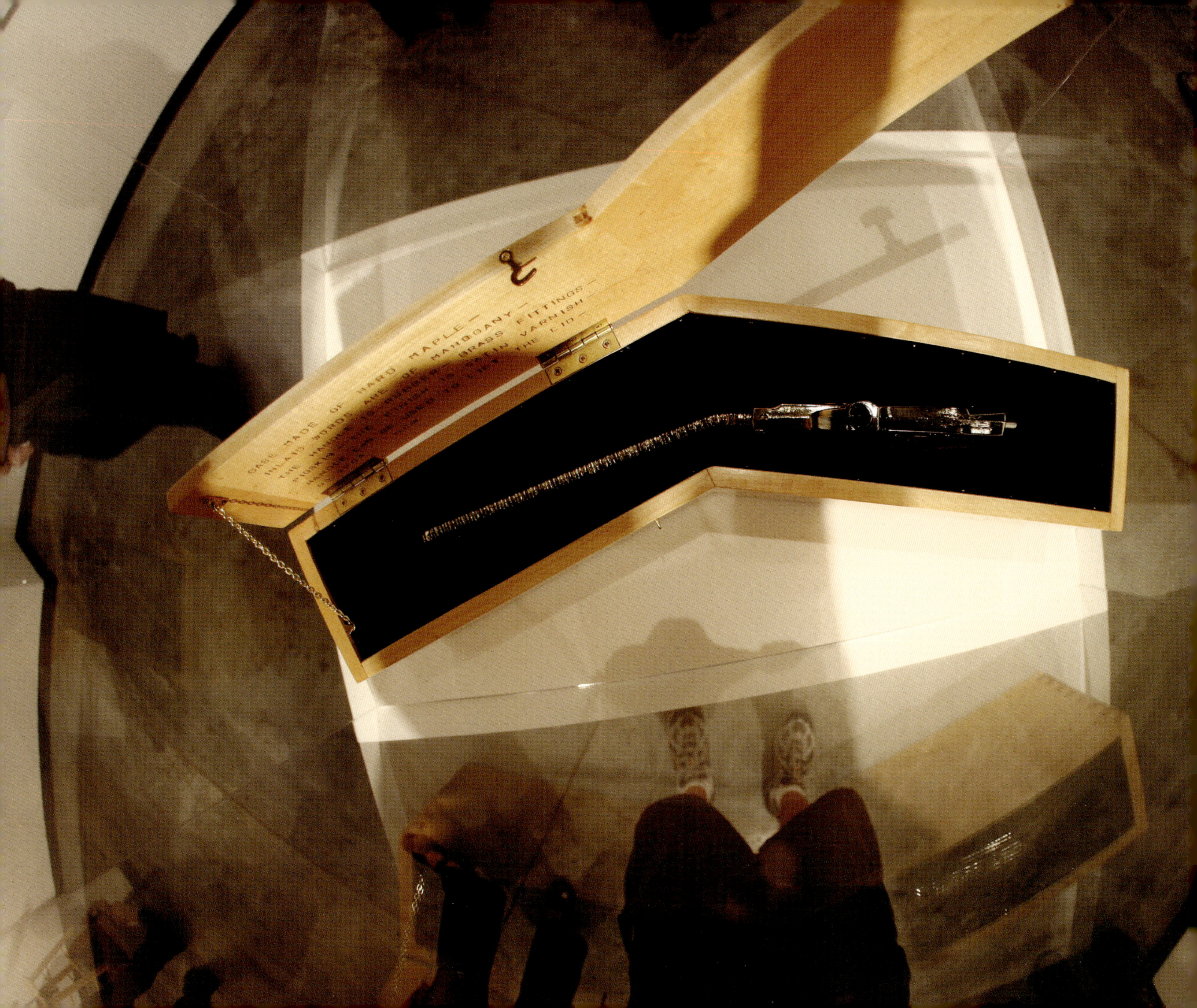
CASE MADE OF HARD MAPLE —
HANDLE CAN BE USED TO LIFT THE LID —

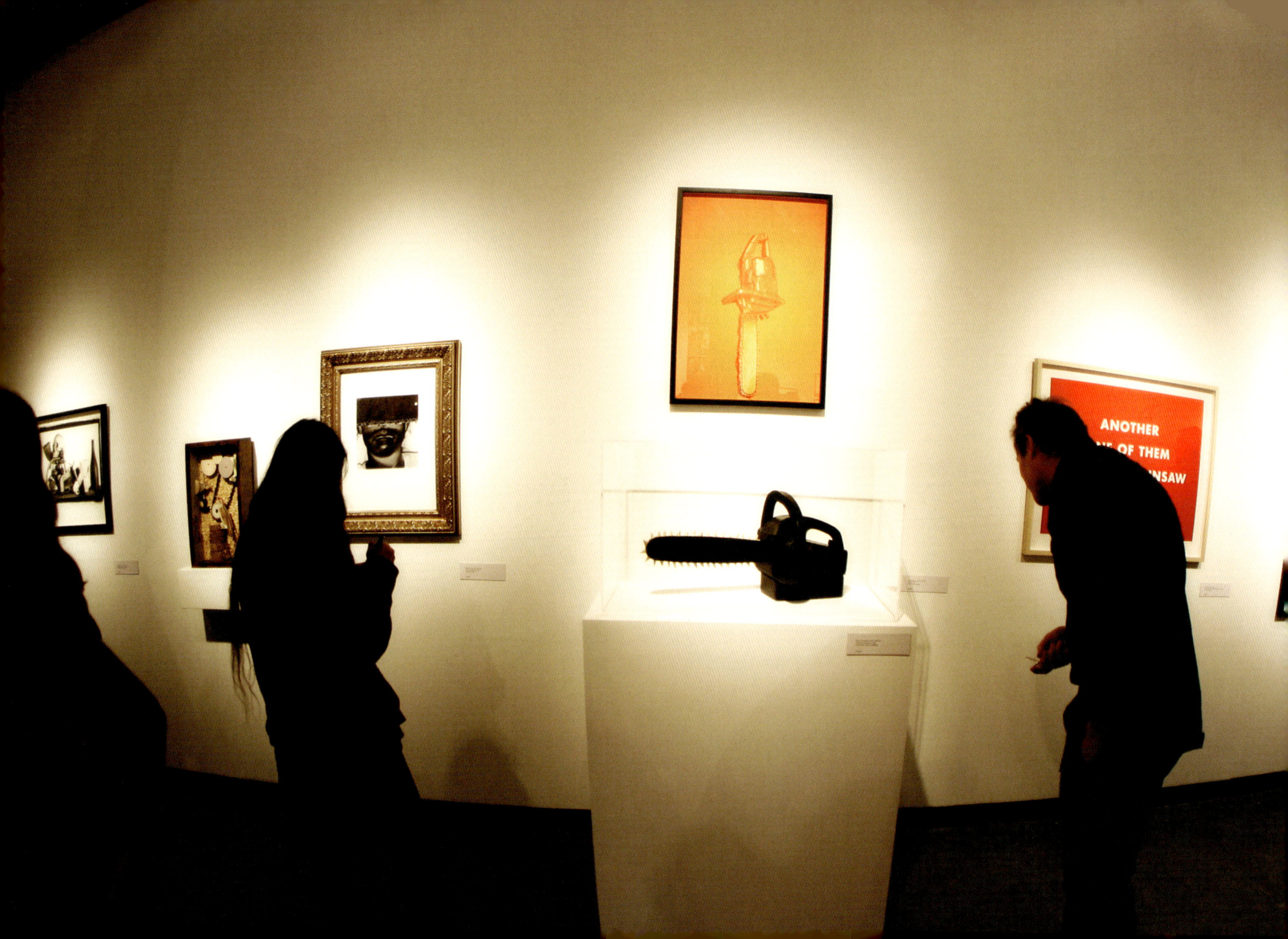
ANOTHER
OF THEM

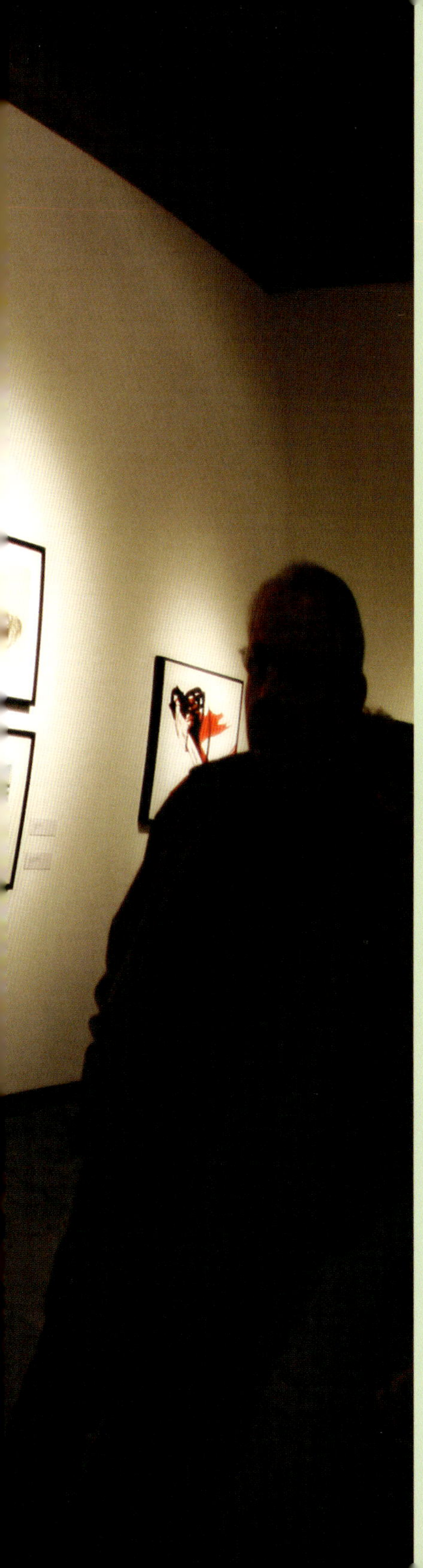

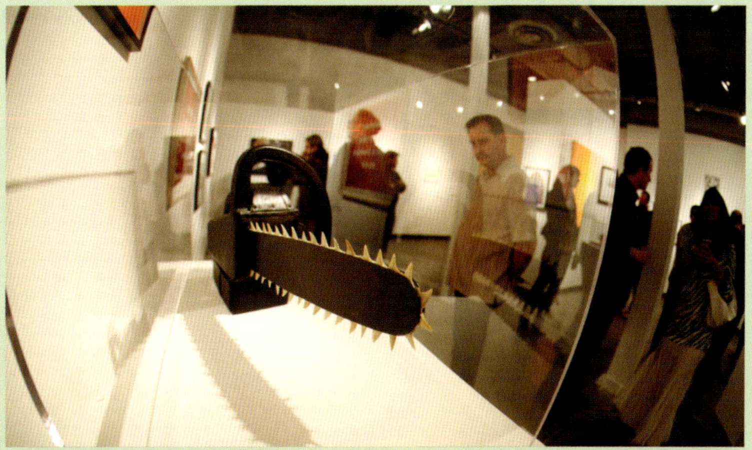

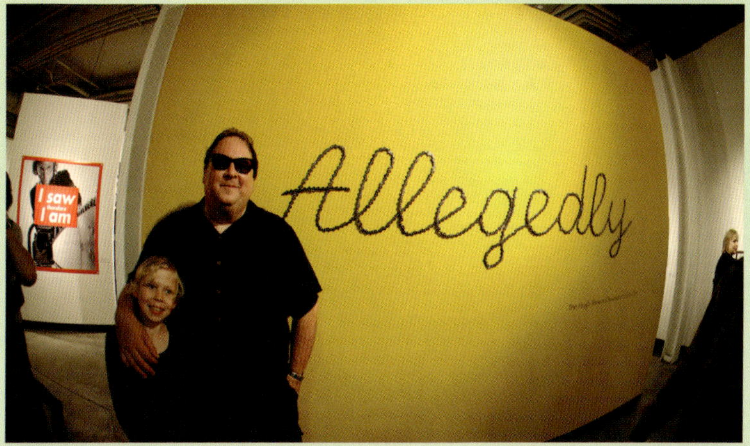
Allegedly

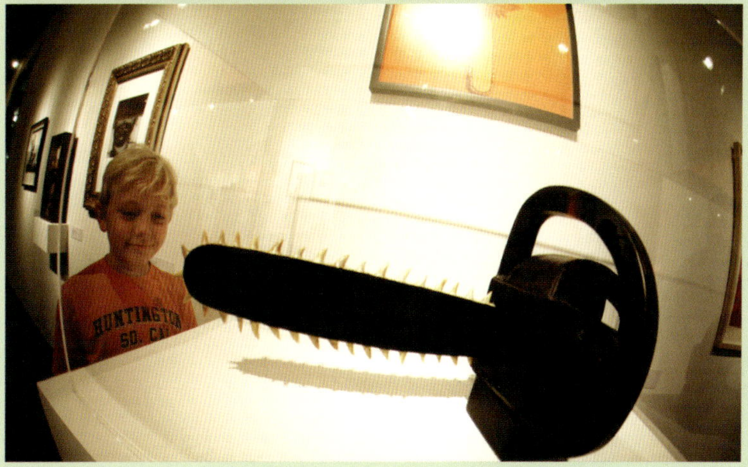

Aiders & Abetters

Aiders — Thanks to Pam & Jim Elyea at History for Hire, JR, Rob, Mike and Senior at G2, Jeff Wasserman and Kevin Giffen at Wasserman Silk Screen, Russell Adams at Schulman Photographic, Ronnie Eisenberg, Victor Boghossian, Alan Forney, Thai and Phillip at Framing House Design, Aldo at Kodak Image Center, Robert Dean, Mary Dean, Ed Ruscha, Tom Sachs, Peter Walberg, and Robin Lewis West.

Abetters — Thanks to Jane Friedman, Ricky Jay, Anne Litt & Howard Franklin, Jerry Stahl, Johanna Went & Stuart Cornfeld, Lori Friedman, Annie Adjchavanich, and Kristine McKenna.

Instigators — Big Thanks to Greg Escalante, Andrea Harris, Dennis Cubbage,and Mike McGee without whom…

Known Associates — Biggest thanks to Liz and Claire, who gave up all household horizontal surfaces for most of the year, Jon Rubin, and accomplice Andy Strauss – studio lender, gaffer, photographer, large canvas hauler, storage finder, and lint wrangler.

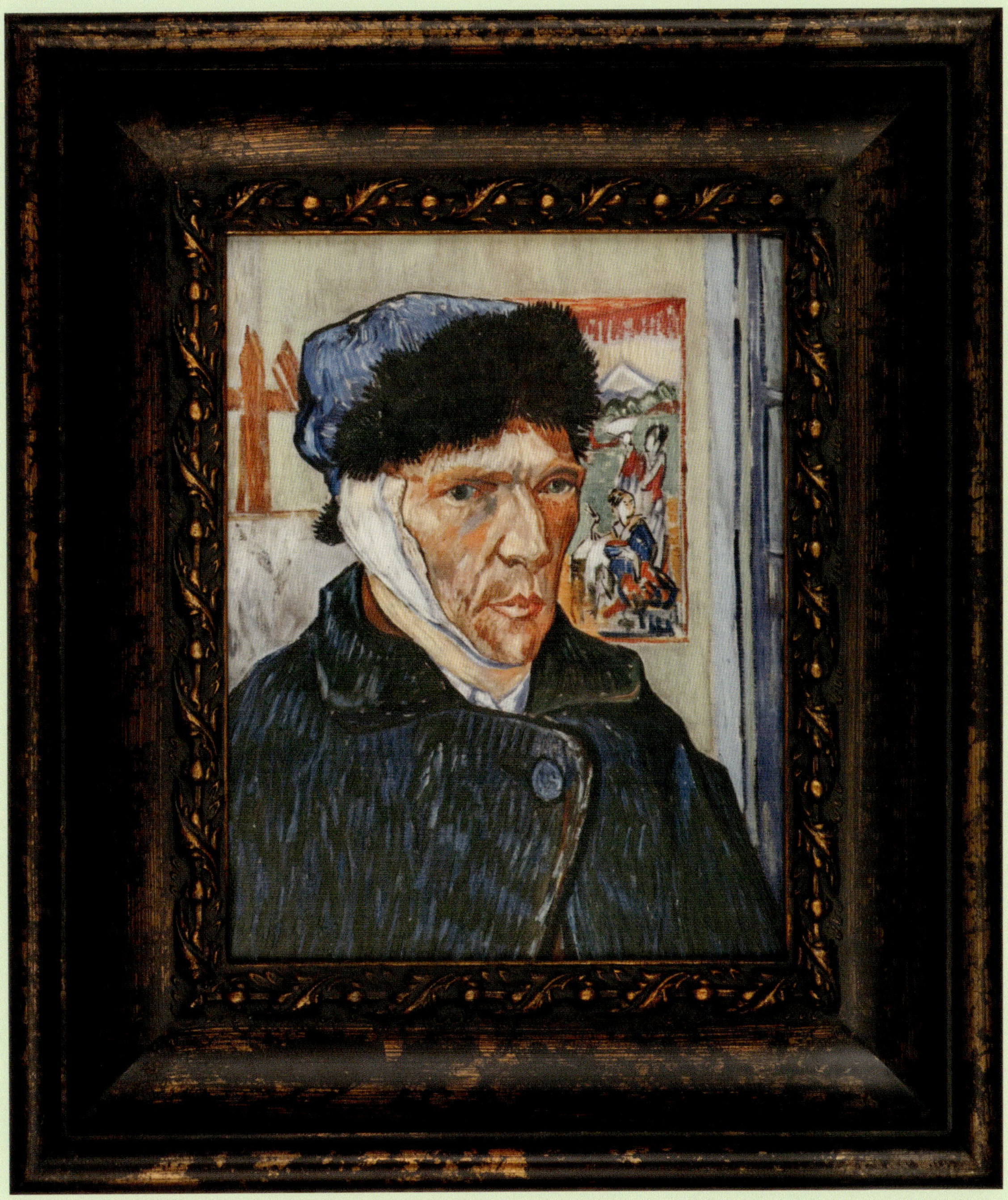

In their book *Van Gogh's Ear: Paul Gauguin and the Pact of Silence*, German academics Hans Kaufmann and Rita Wildegans say that the accepted theory that Van Gogh cut off his own ear is based entirely on Gauguin's statements. They argue that Gauguin, an expert fencer, lopped off the ear during an argument. Van Gogh never talked about it, although he dropped hints in letters to his brother Theo, once commenting: "Luckily Gauguin…is not yet armed with machine guns, chainsaws,* and other dangerous war weapons."

**ink smudged; forensically reconstructed*

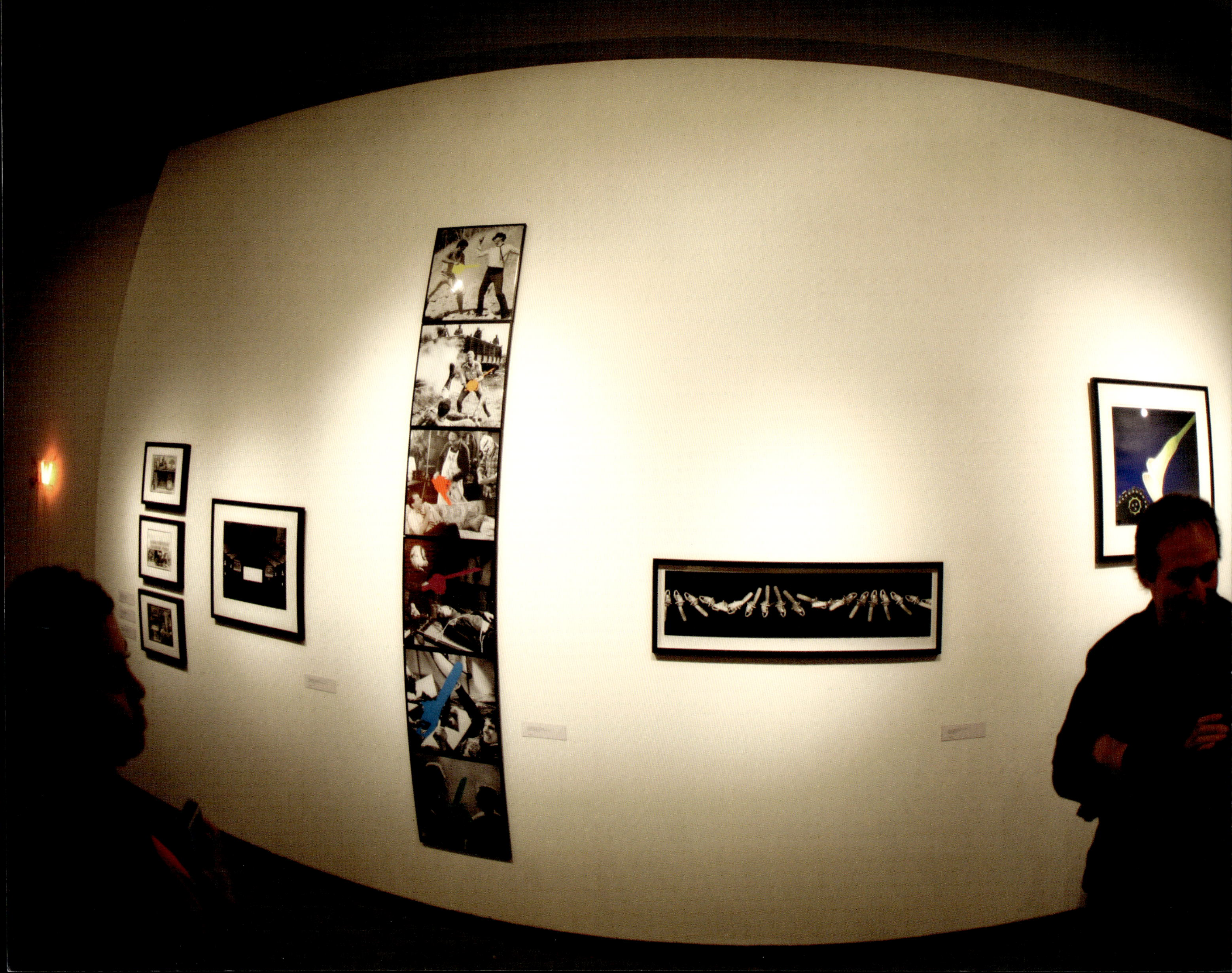

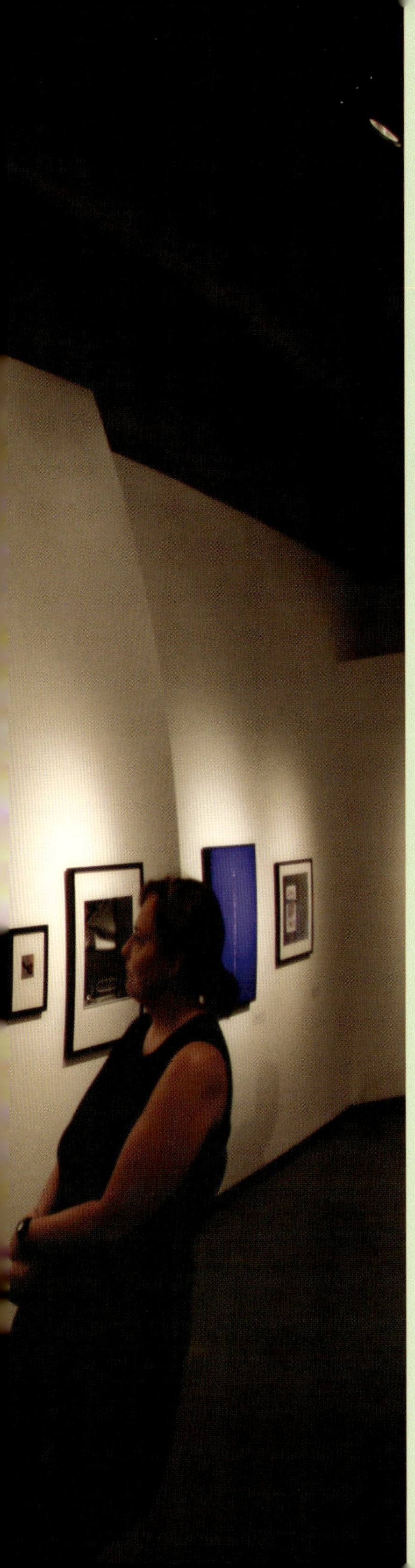

This book is published by: California State University Fullerton Grand Central Art Center and the Grand Central Press. This book has been published in conjunction with the exhibition *Allegedly: The Hugh Brown Chainsaw Collection* for the Grand Central Art Center Gallery, Santa Ana, California, where it was presented 2 May – 14 June 2009

Book Design — Wendy Peng in collaboration with Hugh Brown
Design Consultant — Andrea Harris McGee
Exhibition Curators — Dennis Cubbage in collaboration with Hugh Brown
Editor — Sue Henger
Photography — Hugh Brown, Andy Strauss (pg.77)
Installation images — Eric Stoner
Printed by — Permanent Printing Limited, China

First Printing December 2009

California State University Fullerton Grand Central Art Center
Dennis Cubbage, Tracey Gayer, Alyssa Cordova, Krystal Glasman, Yevgeniya Mikhailik and Matthew William Miller

Grand Central Art Forum
Greg Escalante, Steve Jones, Mitchell De Jarnett, Wendy Sherman, Marcus Bastida, Teri Brudnack, Jon Gothold, John Gunnin, James Hill, Diana Donaldson, Mary Ellen Houseal, Julie Perlin-Lee, Jon Webb, Dennis Lluy, Mike McGee, Robert Redding, G. Ray Kerciu, Shelley Liberto, Chris Hoff, Andrea Harris-McGee, C.W. West, Gil Marrero and Stuart Spence, Advisory members: Peter Alexander, Rose Apodaca Jones, Kristine Escalante, Mike Salisbury, Anton Segerstrom, and Paul Zaloom

California State University Fullerton
President Milton Gordon, Joe Arnold, Marilyn Moore, Marty Lorigan and Bill Dickerson

Grand Central Press
CSUF Grand Central Art Center
125 N. Broadway Santa Ana, California 92701
714-567-7233 714-567-7234
www.grandcentralartcenter.com

Hugh Brown
www.sawmeister.com

ISBN — 978-0-9817987-2-1

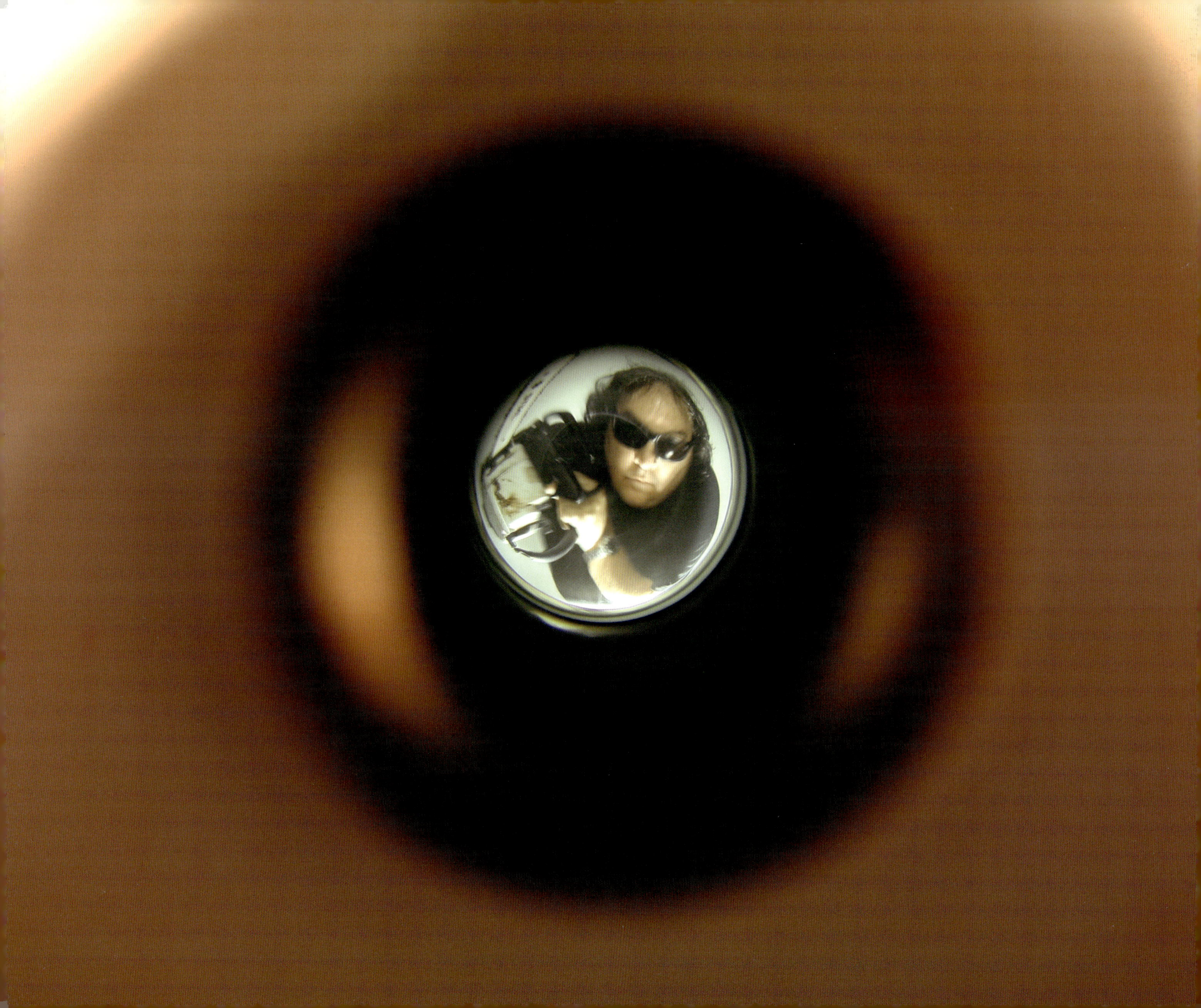